THE LEAGUE OF NATIONS AND THE FORESHADOWING OF THE INTERNATIONAL MONETARY FUND

The very phrase "League of Nations" is a metaphor for international organizational failure. In the wake of the war it was designed to prevent, the League became the example to be avoided in building new multilateral institutions. Perhaps it is not surprising, then, that our textbooks on international relations and international economics leave the impression that the multilateral organizations established after World War II represented entirely new departures in history. This essay aims to refute that impression by examining important and commonly forgotten links between the League and the International Monetary Fund (IMF).

Despite the well-documented contribution of the British delegation at the 1944 Bretton Woods Conference, and the less well known input of the Canadians, the now-conventional view is that the IMF inevitably reflected a fresh and novel American vision for international monetary and financial relations. In this and other policy areas, the title of Dean

I became interested in this topic during a visit to the archives of the League in Geneva a couple of years ago. Having just left the staff of the International Monetary Fund, I was struck by certain similarities between the work of the League and the later work of the Fund. I subsequently approached Jacques Polak, who had long been thinking about the same theme but had not written systematically about it. Without implicating him in what follows, especially in certain of my conclusions that he would undoubtedly view with skepticism, I am happy to record my gratitude for his encouragement. On the same theme, I also interviewed Louis Rasminsky at length. Related conversations with Joseph Gold over many years have been exceptionally helpful. In addition, Mark Allen, James Boughton, Robert Bryce, Ralph Bryant, Edward Bernstein, William Dale, Jacques de Larosière, André de Lattre, Margaret Garritsen de Vries, Wendy Dobson, Bernard Drabble, Wolfgang Duchatczek, Richard Erb, David Finch, Martin Gilman, Manuel Guitián, Marcel Massé, Christopher McMahon, Jeremy Morse, Yoshio Okubo, Sylvia Ostry, Eckard Pieske, Klaus Regling, Wolfgang Riecke, Robert Russell, Eisuke Sakakibara, Aurel Schubert, Robert Solomon, Susan Strange, Andre Szász, Maxwell Watson, H. Johannes Witteveen, and Edwin Yeo gave me the benefit of their views on multilateral economic surveillance and its evolution. For constructive comments on this essay, I am especially grateful to David Andrews, Benjamin Cohen, Stephen Gill, Eric Helleiner, Harold James, Miles Kahler, Evert Lindquist, Michael Webb, and an anonymous reviewer. David McIver provided research assistance. The Social Sciences and Humanities Research Council of Canada and an International Affairs Fellowship from the Council on Foreign Relations supported the project.

Acheson's memoirs, *Present at the Creation*, seems to sum up the worldview of a generation of American policymakers and scholars (Ikenberry, 1992). The global conflagration that began in the 1930s erased what had gone before. The Americans, with a little help from their friends, were painting on a blank canvass.

The United States was, indeed, more than the first among equals after the war, but it is not the case that the postwar experiment in international economic institution building was entirely new. Largely forgotten now is the economic work of the League of Nations. We need to recover that memory, for as we shall see, the monetary and financial activities of the League foreshadowed the core mandate of the IMF as it developed over time. The League's economic activities also influenced the shaping of the IMF mandate in surprisingly direct ways. For this and other reasons, the evolution of those activities in the face of increasingly severe constraints continues to warrant study by those interested in the future of multilateralism in this field.

Research Context

It is widely believed today that free and open capital markets exert a salutary discipline on national economic policies. The true extent of international capital movements remains debatable, but there is little doubt that since the 1970s, a rising tide of national policies has vastly enhanced the potential mobility of capital. Keynes' (1933) famous admonition that finance is not one of those "things which should by their nature be international" seems ever more anachronistic.

In such an environment, it is easy to forget that leading states learned long ago about the importance of mediating market discipline—through international institutions, if not through national political structures. In the mid-1970s, as states struggled to legalize the *de facto* regime of managed exchange rates within the context of freer international capital flows, they enshrined that mediating function in an expanded and formalized IMF mandate for multilateral surveillance. In the United States, even the strongly pro-market, Republican administration of the day assigned a very high priority to the ratification of an amendment to the Fund's Articles of Agreement that gave the IMF responsibility for "firm surveillance" over members' exchange-rate policies (Pauly, 1992, pp. 317–318).[1]

---

[1] On a continuum of policy responses to pressures unleashed by increasing openness (ranging from national autonomy to mutual recognition of national standards and practices,

ESSAYS IN INTERNATIONAL FINANCE

No. 201, December 1996

THE LEAGUE OF NATIONS AND THE FORESHADOWING OF THE INTERNATIONAL MONETARY FUND

LOUIS W. PAULY

INTERNATIONAL FINANCE SECTION

DEPARTMENT OF ECONOMICS
PRINCETON UNIVERSITY
PRINCETON, NEW JERSEY

INTERNATIONAL FINANCE SECTION
EDITORIAL STAFF

Peter B. Kenen, *Director*
Margaret B. Riccardi, *Editor*
Lillian Spais, *Editorial Aide*
Lalitha H. Chandra, *Subscriptions and Orders*

Library of Congress Cataloging-in-Publication Data

Pauly, Louis W.
  The League of Nations and the foreshadowing of the International Monetary Fund /
Louis Pauly.
    p. cm. — (Essays in international finance, ISSN 0071-142X ; no. 201)
  Includes bibliographical references.
  ISBN 0-88165-108-7
    1. International finance. 2. Economic stabilization. 3. League of Nations. Economic
and Financial Section. 4. International Monetary Fund. I. Title. II. Series.
[HG136.P7 no. 201]
[HG3881]
332′.042 s—dc21
[332′.042]   96-51079
                                                                              CIP

Printed in the United States of America by Princeton University Printing Services at
Princeton, New Jersey

International Standard Serial Number: 0071-142X
International Standard Book Number: 0-88165-108-7
Library of Congress Catalog Card Number: 96-51079

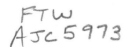

CONTENTS

As Harold James (1996) emphasizes in his excellent history of the IMF, an exchange rate in itself reflects a large number of choices made about national economic policy, including choices about financial and monetary management and openness to capital movements. Even without the Fund's having formal responsibility for overseeing national capital accounts, therefore, the exercise of its refurbished mandate during the past two decades effectively interposed the IMF between burgeoning international capital markets and national political authorities (Strange, 1973; Guitián, 1992a, 1992b). In practice, the Fund's surveillance role entails obligatory consultations with its members, which concentrate on the external implications of a full range of national economic policies. It also includes regular analysis of systemic outcomes as those policies interact under conditions of deepening interdependence. Having evolved from practical experience since the earliest days of the IMF, the Fund's surveillance mandate now underpins all of its more visible activities, including its conditional-financing operations.[2]

The assignment of such a mandate to an international organization was not, however, truly novel. The League of Nations was, in this respect, a direct precursor to the Fund, and the economic and financial work of the League provides insight into the impetus and limits of contemporary practice in the IMF. The League's halting and often frustrating engagement in the incipient practice of national and systemic oversight reminds us that it is no easy matter to build a stable world economy on the foundation of global financial markets. More specifically, it reminds us that the promise of automaticity in the interstate economic adjustments widely associated with the operation of those markets is an illusion. Stable, well-functioning markets that span discrete political jurisdictions must themselves rest on a foundation of political collaboration. In practical terms, given the continuing exigencies of national political independence and national structural distinctiveness—even in this age

---

monitored decentralization, formal policy coordination, explicit harmonization, and federalist mutual governance), multilateral economic surveillance would exist in the political space between monitored decentralization and formal coordination (Cooper, 1989; Dobson, 1991; Solomon, 1991; Kahler, 1995; Kenen, 1995; Bryant, 1995, 1996).

[2] James (1995, pp. 763–764)) contends that "the substance of surveillance was already adumbrated in the early wartime discussions between John Maynard Keynes and Harry Dexter White about the shape of the postwar currency order. In particular, the notion of discretionary management of the international monetary system by a supervisory body was introduced by the United States in order to avoid the potentially very high liabilities implied in Keynes' original vision of an almost completely automatic operating clearing union."

3

of "globalization"—this means that the space between state policy and market reality requires institutional buffers.[3] Such a conclusion was drawn from the painful experience of the League, and it continues to shape the central mandate of the IMF.

No linear or progressive evolutionary process connects the surveillance function of the IMF and its rough analogue in the League. There are, however, some surprisingly direct links and fascinating parallels, especially between the 1920s (the more successful decade of the League's economic career) and the present period.[4] Both eras find political power dispersed among a number of leading states, and international financial markets as the chief transmitter of economic pressures across those states (Helleiner, 1994; Webb, 1995). Such circumstances require that states support those markets, not just with agreed upon principles, but also with collaborative policies mediated by some sort of multilateral institution. During the 1930s, when states failed to meet such a requirement, the point was reinforced the hard way.

The economic experience of the League illustrates the commonly forgotten interaction of states and markets under conditions of, first, deepening integration and principled agreement and, later, disintegration and evident policy disagreement. In both contexts, the interaction underlines the virtues of pragmatism and the fragility of principles that become ideologies. It demonstrates, in addition, the way in which social learning can take place when ideas shaped by painful experience in one institutional setting can be transmitted into another.[5]

[3] The idea that institutions such as the IMF play a buffering role is clear in the vast secondary literature on the subject. Usually, however, analysts have stressed the internal dimension of intermediation, that is, they emphasize the way in which international institutions are enlisted by weak governments to play the role of scapegoat for necessary but unpopular changes in domestic policies. As much as it sometimes pains the IMF, I do not doubt that the IMF often plays such a role, especially when it provides conditional financing. In this essay, however, I emphasize a different kind of buffering role, one that is at least potentially more enduring and more generally applicable. It is, in any event, less commonly examined in the literature.

[4] Barry Eichengreen (1990, p. 3) draws the same analogy: "[In contrast to the pre-World War I period or the post-World War II period,] the interwar period, when policymakers intervened actively in response to conflicts between internal and external balance, more closely resembles the situation that is [today] likely to prevail. Similarly, the trend toward an increasingly multipolar international monetary system is certain to persist into the 21st century. Hence, any new set of institutions will be required to accommodate the objectives of a number of nations possessing roughly comparable financial and monetary resources. The precedent for this situation . . . is the interwar experience."

[5] The case is relevant to themes now being developed in research on the role of ideational consensus at the level of transnational elites, or what some scholars call

The Economic and Financial Organization of the League

The standard history of the League of Nations barely mentions its economic activities (Walters, 1952).[6] This lacuna may be partly explained by the fact that the original architects of the League never explicitly intended such activities to develop (Hill, 1945, p. 15).[7] Only Articles 22 and 23 of the League's Covenant actually mention economic matters, and then, only in very specific contexts.[8] That a set of formal committees, special councils, and a secretariat began to develop on this

---

"epistemic communities." See, for example, Odell, 1988; Hall, 1989; Adler and Haas, 1992; Goldstein and Keohane, 1993; Ikenberry, 1993; and Yee, 1996.

[6] The subject is also given short shrift in more recent histories, including those by George Scott (1973) and F.S. Northedge (1986). This is especially curious in light of evidence that economic factors were much in the minds of those whose ideas helped spawn the League. Norman Angell, for example, wrote extensively and passionately about the economic underpinnings of the post-World War I peace. Angell was blunt about his agenda, and it is known that he had a direct personal influence on Colonel House and President Wilson (Scott, 1973, p. 17). He saw economic conflicts as contributing to past and likely future wars. He noted England's "special dependence" on an orderly world. He saw the power and authority over economic matters wielded by the Inter-Allied Economic Commissions during the Great War as contradicting the orthodox argument that rational guidance of economic forces was impossible. He insisted that if governments did not lead that process, "great international trusts" would. He concluded that the way ahead lay in the construction of "super-national" authorities (Angell, 1920). For a recent political analysis of international organizations that includes a relevant overview of the work of the League, see Murphy, 1994.

[7] Martin Hill's study is an extraordinarily useful and detailed memoir, apparently drafted at the behest of the Carnegie Endowment in light of the then-raging debate over the structure of international institutions after the war. Another useful reference, albeit one that only covers the early period, is McClure, 1933. Wallace McClure was a member of the U.S. Department of State, and his lengthy and exhaustively documented history ends just prior to the World Economic Conference of 1933.

[8] Article 22 aimed to establish equal conditions for trade in territories placed under League mandate, and Article 23e, harking back to the principle of nondiscrimination codified in the Cobden-Chevalier Treaty of 1860, declared "equitable treatment for the commerce of all members of the League" (Dunham, 1930, pp. 141–142; Ratcliffe, 1973; Cottrell, 1974). The original American draft of the Covenant included an amplification of the third of Woodrow Wilson's famous Fourteen Points: that every nation should be free to adopt and change its system of export and import duties and prohibitions, but "every such system . . . shall . . . as to the rest of the world be equal and without discrimination, difference, or preference, direct or indirect." Because no consensus could be reached on this principle, justification for the later economic activities of the League always rested on the preamble of the Covenant, which highlighted the general objective "to promote international co-operation and to achieve international peace and security . . . by the prescription of open, just and honorable relations between nations" (Hill, 1945, pp. 15–16).

basis testifies less to their legal foundation than to the nature of the problems encountered by member states in the years following the Armistice. Functions developed from practice as specific tasks were assigned to the League by its leading members.

Part of the League's secretariat evolved into an "Economic, Financial, and Transit Department (Section)." Walter Layton and, then, Frank Nixon were the first directors, soon to be followed by Arthur Salter, who served as permanent director from 1922 until 1931. All were British nationals, as was the League's secretary general, Eric Drummond. Members of the department in the early years included Jean Monnet from France, Per Jacobsson from Sweden, and Alexander Loveday from Britain, who headed the self-contained Economic Intelligence Service (Monnet, 1978; Erin Jacobsson, 1979). The department was split in 1931 into various components, with Loveday taking over the financial and economic intelligence work and Pietro Stoppani of Italy leading the economic section. In 1938, all of the sections were joined together again under Loveday.

The staff worked under the broad guidance of the League's assembly, which included a few ministers of commerce and finance, and the more specific direction of standing committees of the council, which was mainly comprised of foreign ministers. Economic, financial, fiscal, and statistical committees were established, and all later operated separately or jointly. This meant that the work of the staff was not always clearly circumscribed. Although some staff members worked mainly on what we would today call macroeconomic issues, many moved fluidly across policy terrain that is now split between such organizations as the IMF, the World Bank, and the World Trade Organization (WTO). In addition, and often quite extensively, outside experts and special-purpose committees complemented the work of the staff. Prior to World War II, sixty-five League staffers worked exclusively on economic and financial matters, and their operations became known as the Economic and Financial Organization (EFO) of the League.[9] Almost all of these staff members worked in Geneva until the summer of 1940, when forty took up residence at the Institute for Advanced Study in Princeton, New Jersey.

Much as their descendants in the IMF portray themselves today, spokesmen for the EFO always presented themselves as "technicians"

[9] The largest of the League's technical arms, the EFO was distinct from, but in some ways complementary to, the separately established International Labour Office. By way of comparison, the separate organizations for health, communications and transit, drug control, and social questions never employed, all together, more than sixty staff members.

involved in "technical" problems. The actual mandate of the EFO proved to be expansive and profoundly political, however, just as the Fund's mandate would be later. Perhaps for this reason, the work was perceived by many to be simultaneously exhilarating and frustrating. As the first director of the EFO remarked to his successor in 1922, "the chances of its [the EFO's] being able to do any really useful work [are] so poor that it should be reduced to the smallest dimensions and put into cold storage for an indefinite time" (Salter, 1961, pp. 174–175). Many years later, Louis Rasminsky, who joined the EFO in 1930 and played a significant role in establishing the IMF during the next decade, put the matter more prosaically: "At the League, we were expected to catch fish, but we had no bait" (personal interview, Ottawa, August 11, 1992). Between the early 1920s and the early 1930s, however, there were times of hope, even of optimism.

Liberal Dreams: The Brussels Conference and the Inception of Multilateral Oversight

The seeds of multilateral economic oversight, the incipient mandate of the organization that would become the EFO, were sown in Brussels during the International Financial Conference of 1920. The economies of Europe were then in extreme distress. Industrial and agricultural production had been devastated by the war and its chaotic aftermath; trade was being throttled as bankrupt governments raised tariffs in a desperate attempt to raise revenues and protect domestic producers. Banking systems were in disarray; foreign credit was inadequate to stimulate the process of reconstruction; and ruinous inflationary spirals had been unleashed. In these circumstances, thirty-nine countries answered the League's call for a conference to consider the impasse and suggest solutions. Delegates, although nominated by their governments, were to attend in their private capacities.[10] This maneuver testified to the immensity of the task, from which governments desired some distance, but it also allowed for the attendance of delegates from nonmember countries, including the United States.[11]

---

[10] Mainly prominent bankers and business leaders were involved. Their reports were backed by studies commissioned from the most eminent economists of the day, including Gustav Cassel, A. C. Pigou, Charles Gide, and Maffeo Pantaleoni.

[11] The involvement of the United States in the actual day-to-day work of the League is a story in itself. Suffice it to recall an anecdote related by Polak, who was on the staff of the League from 1938 to 1943. Strolling the cavernous halls of the League's head-quarters one day just after his arrival, Polak came upon an office humming with activity.

7

In retrospect, it is easy to downplay the results of the Brussels Conference. With no substantive authority, the declarations of its expert groups were obviously hortatory. Nonetheless, the delegates reached a remarkably broad consensus on the principles appropriate for guiding national policies. The delegates appealed to governments to return to the internal policy goals of the prewar era. Governments should balance their budgets and restore credibility to their currencies by disinflating. "The country which accepts the policy of budget deficits," the delegates collectively intoned in words that reverberate today, "is treading the slippery slope to general ruin; to escape from that path, no sacrifice is too great" (International Financial Conference, 1920, p. 10). Not so often heard today, however, is the corollary:

> To enable governments to give effect to the principle of sound finance, all classes of the community must contribute their share. All classes of the population and particularly the wealthy must be prepared willingly to accept the charges necessary to remedy the present situation. . . . Fresh taxation must be imposed to meet the deficit (International Financial Conference, 1920, pp. 11–12).

The conference also called for a drastic reduction in expenditures on armaments, then still averaging 20 percent of national budgets.

With regard to exchange rates, most histories of the conference have reported an appeal for a return to the gold standard. It is true that delegates cited the stability associated with a viable gold standard as representing an ideal to be achieved. They stated, however, that a return to the gold standard should not be attempted before countries were ready, before internal financial stability was established.[12] The delegates made other recommendations, including one calling for the abolition of "artificial" restraints on trade. Finally, they requested the secretariat of the League to issue a report on the actual responses of governments to all of their recommendations.

His curiosity piqued, he was later told what "everyone" knew. The office belonged to a permanent "adviser" to the League from the U.S. Department of State (personal interview, Washington, D.C., September 19, 1994). Note that the post-World War II economic institutions would be developed under the auspices of the U. S. Treasury Department.

[12] Without a basis in "sound" domestic policies, "devaluation and deflation would be needed, but this could be disastrous. [We therefore] do not recommend any attempt to stabilize the value of gold and gravely doubt whether such an attempt could succeed. [We believe further] that neither an international currency nor an international unit of account would serve any useful purpose or remove any of the difficulties from which international exchange suffers today" (International Financial Conference, 1920, p. 13).

That report was released in 1922 (League of Nations, 1922). Drafted on the basis of a coherent set of principles, it set down an important marker. No leap of imagination is required to see in it the precursor of the world economic surveys now regularly compiled and published by the IMF and its sister agencies in fulfillment of their own systemic oversight roles. In light of the events of the 1930s, it is easy to be cynical about the utility of the 1922 report and the process that initiated it. But how was it viewed by contemporaries? As one close observer recalled twenty-five years after the Brussels Conference:

> The recommendations exercised a powerful influence on governments and expert opinion in the ensuing years; they were applied by the League in its various schemes for the financial reconstruction of individual countries; they also provided a standard of financial orthodoxy to which appeal was constantly made in the course of the subsequent painful and difficult process of restoring budgetary and currency stability and reopening the channels of international trade. This was the real achievement of the Conference (Hill, 1945, p. 22).

What really matters, however, is not what governments said, but what they did. In the 1920s, they would at least try to put the principles into practice. As we shall see, this meant attempting to reassure international markets and to steer their operation in a constructive direction. Although the League was not the instigator of that attempt, it became a central instrument in its pursuit.

Developing Core Principles: The Genoa Conference of 1922

As is true today with the IMF, the oversight function of the League initiated by the Brussels Conference took two distinct forms. The first was analytical and balanced; symmetry was sought in the rhetorical application of principled guidance to all countries.[13] The second applied those principles more forcefully. It finds its contemporary analogue in the conditionality applied to countries seeking financial support from the IMF (Guitián, 1981; Polak, 1991). A few Central European countries confronted something similar in the early 1920s. Before turning to those cases, however, we need to consider the elaboration of the Brussels principles at the first major postwar economic conference attended by heads of government.

[13] In the 1922 report, code words were often used to express core principles (much as contemporary IMF surveys speak of "fiscal consolidation" and "monetary stabilization"). Everyone understood what the words meant, however, and what principles lay behind them.

At the Paris Peace Conference in January 1922, the principal Allied powers invited the heads of government of the former Axis powers and the Soviet Union to meet at Genoa the following April to resolve economic and financial issues that had not been addressed by the Armistice. Because the Genoa Conference was not technically held under the auspices of the League of Nations, the formal participation of the United States and the Soviet Union was permitted.[14] Although there were noteworthy economic items in the conference agenda, all coordinated by the secretariat of the League, the most important among them were deeply intertwined with vital questions of military security.[15]

In the end, the Genoa Conference would come to signify the beginning of the end of the League's collective-security experiment. It nevertheless managed to adopt three major reports submitted by special commissions of the League. The reports concerned economic, financial, and transportation issues and took the form of wide-ranging overviews. Didactic in style and liberal in tone, they contained numerous recommendations for reforms in government policies.[16] For our purposes, the most interesting report was that of the Financial Commission.

---

[14] Britain's prime minister, Lloyd George, was particularly chary of making the conference a League event. As he explained with some prescience before the conference:

> [Some] think that the Genoa Conference should have been left to the League of Nations. I am a believer in the League of Nations. . . . Yet you must not run a thing like this too hard. . . . The League of Nations is in the making. You cannot make these things by written constitutions. You must create confidence in them; and confidence can only be created by achievement, and every failure . . . at this stage is a ruinous one. It is like the fall of an infant; it might result in a broken spine and the infant simply limp for the rest of its days (McClure, 1933, pp. 214–215).

[15] If the plans of Lloyd George had borne fruit, the conference would have ratified a British commitment to the territorial integrity of France, to French concessions on the issue of German reparations, and to a joint European-American agreement on the financial reconstruction of the Soviet Union. In the annals of the interwar period, however, the conference stands out as a diplomatic disaster of the first rank. The profound ideological cleavage between the Soviet delegation and the main sponsors was by now undeniable, and the highly emotional reparations issue poisoned the atmosphere. Most famously, the Soviet and German delegations seized the opportunity to take a side trip to the nearby resort of Rapallo to negotiate a separate peace. In the end, none of the critical issues was settled, and most were further complicated.

[16] The liberal tone was not always as "orthodox" as is commonly depicted. The report of the Economic Commission, for example, pushed for the maximum limitation of restraints on trade, but it reserved nice phrases for certain kinds of government intervention, including "the development of public works in aid of unemployment." Unanimity was obtained on many, but not all, issues. A recommendation supporting the most-favored-nation principle in trading relations, for example, was not unanimously supported (Mills, 1922).

The Financial Commission's report elaborated on the principles first articulated two years earlier in Brussels (McClure, 1933, pp. 213–214). Instead of concentrating on the internal macroeconomic requirements for financial stabilization, however, it concentrated on the microeconomic foundations of economic recovery and growth. The Financial Commission was headed by the British chancellor of the exchequer, and its report bore the marks of the principal commissioners, all leading British, American, German, Dutch, or Swedish bankers.

The report called for an end to "futile and mischievous" exchange controls. It decried political interference in the business of banking and called for greater autonomy for central banks. It recommended cooperation among those banks on a range of issues, most importantly on recovering a monetary role for gold. The report proposed a novel plan for restoring a version of the gold standard without unduly impairing world liquidity: the strongest countries would hold their reserves in gold, whereas others could hold reserves in the convertible currencies of the strongest countries.[17] The report also recommended a thorough study by the League of the interrelated issues of capital flight, tax evasion, and double taxation. Finally, it opposed, in principle, intergovernmental loans or governmentally sponsored debt write-offs and advocated private refinancing of existing governmental debts. Exactly how this could be done, given the politically untenable weight of outstanding Soviet debt and German reparations obligations, was left unspecified.[18]

These recommendations did not, of course, stand alone, and there were reasons more profound than ideology for their orthodoxy. Conceptually and politically, there was no way that the restoration of the freer flow of international commerce could occur in the absence of stable currency markets. Beyond having governments enshrine the

---

[17] Keynes covered the conference as a special correspondent for the *Manchester Guardian*. His contribution included publication of his own scheme for a gold-exchange standard allowing for limited fluctuations in exchange rates and backed up financially by the U.S. Federal Reserve. The scheme attracted attention but was stillborn. Keynes would return to the same idea in 1942, when his audience was more receptive (Skidelsky, 1992, pp. 107–108).

[18] Against the backdrop of his famous critique of German reparations, Keynes wrote:

We are asking Russia to repeat words without much caring whether or not they represent sincere intentions, just as we successfully pressed Germany. . . . We act as high priests, not as debt collectors. The heretics must repeat our creed. . . . Genoa, instead of trying to disentangle the endless coil of impossible debt, merely proposes to confuse it further with another heap of silly bonds. The belief that all this protects and maintains the sacredness of contract is the opposite of the truth (Skidelsky, 1992, p. 109).

"sanctity of contracts," no one had any idea how to ensure stability in the wake of the all-too-imaginable defaults that were likely to follow from the Soviets, the Germans, and others.

As became apparent in the debate at Genoa, without the financial stability that was expected to result from a gold-exchange standard and from well-functioning private capital markets, there could be no consensus on the conference report's recommendation that national commercial policies should be reconstituted on the principle of nondiscrimination. France and Spain, in particular, feared that the combination of nondiscriminatory trade policies with capital mobility and the possibility of intentional currency depreciation would devastate their economies. In the words of one observer, "the pervasive factor of currency instability was mainly responsible for the continued enforcement of import prohibitions and restrictions in many European countries, those with weak currencies seeking thereby to strengthen their balance of payments position, the others anxious to guard against exchange dumping" (Hill, 1945, p. 35). Export controls to protect agricultural supplies and raw materials had a similar effect. It was clear that financial stability must come first, and on that, the conference achieved consensus.

The fundamental dilemma, however, remained intractable. With no shared understanding of the principled foundations for compatible commercial policies, it would never be clear that financial stabilization—even if it could be engineered through private financial markets—would initiate a virtuous cycle of reconstruction and growth across Europe. Without such a consensus, it would continue to be logical, even necessary, for countries to husband all possible future bargaining chips on trade and to cooperate with one another only on matters for which an unambiguous domestic rationale existed.[19] Financial stabilization in itself had such a rationale, and few politicians, therefore, would have seen much reason to disrupt the collective understandings of the bankers. Only if and when the bankers failed would governments have to clarify their priorities. Helping them not to fail would therefore be important. The first test would come as various Central European countries approached the financial brink.

[19] As Hill explained in 1945:

In the conditions prevailing in the early twenties, there was little prospect of bringing about concerted action to promote freer and more equal trade. Those conditions were political, financial, and economic in character; and it is important to note that while the political organs of the League were endeavoring to establish security . . . and the Financial Committee was assisting in stabilizing the currencies and reconstructing the finances of individual European countries, there was no means—and no plan—for dealing with the economic [read "political"] causes of the existing state of trade relationships (Hill, 1945, p. 36).

Imperfect though they would prove to be in their broader application, the liberal principles developed in Genoa guided the League as it grappled with the debt crises of the 1920s. The League's incipient role of providing systemic oversight was signified in the background work and final economic reports accepted at Genoa, but little practical effect could be claimed until the opportunity arose to apply the principles of those reports directly in Central Europe.

Applying the Principles: The League and the Financial Reconstruction of Central Europe

The refinancing of Austria in 1923 is usually recorded as the first debt workout involving the League. It was, in fact, the second. According to a memorandum written by a senior League staffer in August 1922, the League had assisted with a loan floated on international capital markets for Czecho-Slovakia earlier that year. To assure repayment, the lead investment banker, Baring Brothers, had demanded the right to control directly the administration of customs and tariff receipts pledged as security, a condition that had earlier been successfully imposed on Turkey. Czecho-Slovakia refused to accede, and a compromise was struck on the basis of its suggestion that the League be appointed as arbitrator in case of future disputes; in the event of difficulty with the loan's security, the League would be empowered to "take such action as might be necessary to secure the interest of the bond holders." The agreement was subsequently ratified by both the lending syndicate (which included a predecessor to the United States' Citibank) and the council of the League. As the League staffer put it: "Evidently, the reason why this kind of arrangement is satisfactory to the government is that Czecho-Slovakia is a member of the League, and she is not therefore sacrificing her independence or diminishing her sovereignty in accepting [League] arbitration" (Nixon, 1922).

As the case of Czecho-Slovakia implies, there were substantial differences in the precise modalities through which funds for economic stabilization could be provided during the early 1920s and in analogous situations today. Unlike the IMF, the League had no funds of its own, and because intergovernmental lending was frowned upon in principle, any significant external financing had to come from private capital markets. In later cases in which the League would be much more actively engaged, its main contribution would be to provide the same sort of political buffer it had supplied for Czecho-Slovakia.

13

In the Austrian case, the country's marketable assets were already encumbered by foreign liens, and the reparations payments imposed in the aftermath of the Armistice were crushing. Hyperinflation was by now institutionalized. As a senior League official noted during his first visit in 1922, office clerks were using Austrian crown notes as scribbling paper. It was the cheapest paper they could get, costing sixty times its face value to print (Salter, 1961, p. 175; see also Dornbusch, 1994; Garber and Spencer, 1994). The broader human consequences are well documented. Famine was widespread, and Austrian society was on the edge of an abyss. In this context, fractious political debate was beginning to center, once again, on the idea that the only road to survival was the one that led to Berlin. The victorious Allies had long ago come to fear just such an outcome. Having vetoed a union in 1919, they subsequently used both public and private charitable routes to pump emergency financing into the Austrian economy.

Britain had built up the largest exposure. By 1922, however, the British, French, and American governments were unwilling to contribute more. The governor of the Bank of England advised the British Cabinet that the effects of total financial collapse in Austria could be contained. The Cabinet agreed "that no useful purpose would be served by advancing additional financial assistance to the Austrian government merely with a view to postponing what appeared to be an inevitable financial catastrophe" (Scott, 1973, p. 80). An inter-Allied conference was convened in London on August 7, and the decision to stop further loans was taken. One additional decision followed. On August 15, the task of dealing with the consequences was handed over to the League (Toynbee, 1925, pp. 321–322). As one historian reflected:

> What the Allied powers seemed to be doing—and probably thought they were doing—was washing their hands of Austria and leaving the League to take whatever opprobrium was going when the country broke up. Prudent voices advised the Council of the League to have nothing to do with it, because the certain failure of Austria must harm the League. But the Council took it on (Scott, 1973, p. 80).[20]

In the event, the council established a special "Austria Committee" comprised of key foreign ministers and the Austrian chancellor. Under its direction, the secretariat worked out a plan of action that elaborated

---

[20] Salter claimed that the push to accept the challenge came from League staff member Jean Monnet, who was convinced that external military intervention by competing powers could be averted if the League grasped the reins of a quintessential collective-action problem (Salter, 1961, p. 178). It is worth noting that Monnet's homeland

a concrete program for currency reform proposed by British treasury officials. The result, after much delay, was a £26,000,000 loan, which was raised in private markets, guaranteed by eight European governments, and administered directly in Vienna by a commissioner appointed by the League. For three and a half years thereafter, this meant that the League commissioner, assisted by Arthur Salter and other members of the secretariat, would personally supervise the flow of customs revenues and other foreign exchange through government coffers (Huber, 1992). Without such oversight, lenders could not be confident that their loan would be repaid.

The memory of Commissioner-General Alfred Zimmerman, a Dutch national and former mayor of Rotterdam, remains remarkably vivid in Austrian financial circles, not so much for his rescue of the Austrian economy as for his lack of tact while doing so. The commissioner's role gave him considerable influence over Austrian economic policy. How could the League ensure that influence would not be perceived as arbitrary? League staff anticipated three prerequisites. Zimmerman's advice would have to be consistent with general principles acknowledged as applicable to all countries; he would have to leave as soon as possible; and he would have to be thoroughly practiced in the arts of diplomacy. In the end, the first two proved sufficient to the specific task.

The basic principles of financial stabilization articulated at the Brussels Conference and developed at Genoa were applied, and the intervention worked, despite Dr. Zimmerman's reported heavy-handedness.[21] Zimmerman left after forty-two months; the loan was repaid; the currency was stabilized; and the national budget was balanced. A process of reconstruction had begun. No one could then predict that it would all collapse in 1931, or that the League itself would be destroyed by the global forces thereby unleashed.

Hailed as the League's first practical achievement, the Austrian loan was followed by another to a desperate Hungary in 1924. Under the terms of a program modeled on the Austrian plan, a £10,000,000

---

had the most to lose if the territorial expansion of Germany, itself unstable, were the end-result of Austria's financial collapse. There is evidence, too, that the assembly and council of the League were moved by emotional pleas from Monsignor Seipel, then Austria's chancellor (Scott, 1973, p. 81).

[21] An American from the Inter-Allied Reparations Commission, Roland Boyden, had almost been appointed in preference to Zimmerman. Salter later blamed Zimmerman's lack of diplomacy for exacerbating internal political conflict between the principal Austrian parties (Salter, 1961, pp. 180–181).

(unguaranteed) infusion accomplished the same result. A League-appointed commissioner effectively acted as the agent for the note holders, administered the program directly in Budapest, and left after two years (Tyler, 1945).

League staff subsequently offered minor technical assistance to Estonia, to the free city of Danzig, and to Portugal,[22] but these later programs seemed to leave a stigma that discouraged others from associating with the League. As Arthur Salter (1961, p. 182) put it, somewhat too delicately:

> By [the late 1920s] the very fame of the League's action entailed disadvantages. It led to the belief that the appropriate clients for the League were countries who were completely down and out and who both needed, and would be required to accept, the same onerous and rather humiliating form of control for a period. Other countries therefore . . . , while profiting from the technical experience gained in the League's experiments, preferred to make direct arrangements with foreign issuing houses and to carry reforms through without any impairment of national responsibility beyond what might be imposed by the lenders.[23]

Substitute "IMF" for "League," and few would be surprised to see Salter's words applied to the contemporary period. Authoritative oversight by a multilateral institution, although preferable to direct intrusion by another state, was (and is) never enthusiastically welcomed by recipients. Nevertheless, as we shall see, a number of countries returned to the League after they sank back into debt crises in the early 1930s. Once again, catastrophe brought to light the need for a collaborative political mechanism to underpin ostensibly private international markets. It also underlined a basic paradox. The actions of

---

[22] League staff were also involved in raising private financing for Greece and Bulgaria when those countries were faced with massive refugee inflows in consequence of local wars. They worked under the direction of the now-formalized Financial Committee of the League, which consisted of officials seconded by the British, French, and Belgian finance ministries, and central bankers, prominent businessmen, and private bankers from Switzerland and Holland. There were also frequent direct contacts between League officials and Montagu Norman of the Bank of England, Benjamin Strong and George Harrison of the U.S. Federal Reserve, Thomas Lamont and Dwight Morrow of J.P. Morgan, and others (Salter, 1961, p. 190).

[23] Salter wanly added, "The Financial Committee was attempting to alter its standard form of association with borrowing countries when the change in the general world situation made an advance upon these lines impracticable" (Salter, 1961, p. 182; also see League of Nations, 1930). For directly relevant analysis of the connection between the weakness of national authorities and the usefulness of buffering by outside agencies, see Santaella, 1993.

states could easily destabilize those markets, but without the sense of confidence only states could provide, the markets could not function at all. In the late 1920s, however, the dream lived on that politics could somehow be removed from the markets.

Liberal Orthodoxy Resurgent: League Oversight at the End of the 1920s

Buoyed by the unexpected successes of the Austrian and Hungarian stabilizations, members of the League's assembly began talking in 1925 of an international conference to address in a holistic fashion the myriad economic problems still plaguing the world. Unlike the Genoa meeting, this conference would be formally sponsored by the League and would concentrate on economic issues. The aim, in short, was to broaden and refine the Genoa consensus on the economic policies required for prosperity. "Economic peace will largely contribute to security among nations," one assembly delegate intoned. The way forward had just been charted by the League itself in Austria and Hungary, and by the recent acceptance of plans to resolve the long-standing reparations question (Clarke, 1967; Schuker, 1988; Simmons, 1993). "Financial reconstruction," the assembly concluded, "is the basis of economic reconstruction" (McClure, 1933, pp. 215–216).[24]

As for the specific goals of the conference, one of its principal supporters, the delegate from France, warned that the meeting would not result in international treaties. Instead, "the Conference would enunciate a number of principles [and] it would seek some method of international cooperation to apply them." In consequence, in certain key sectors, this might bring about agreements among companies with the assent of governments that would ensure "stability of production and consumption" (McClure, 1933, pp. 217–218). In the background, quite evidently, were organized business interests concerned about rising levels of protectionism since the end of the war.[25] "While separate national economies should be taken into consideration," the delegate from Italy held, attention "should be directed toward the great

---

[24] At the same time, as the delegate from France noted in debate, there existed "an astonishing paradox: as money becomes stabilized, economic crises arise. In Germany [for example] monetary stability had prevailed for two years, yet it was immediately followed by an economic crisis" (McClure, 1933, p. 220).

[25] League archives include extensive files dating back to 1920 for correspondence from the International Chamber of Commerce (Box 503, Sec. 10a, 1920).

natural lines of production which did not stop short at frontiers" (McClure, 1933, p. 219).

In the course of preparing an agenda for the conference, League officials came to see that the regulation of trade and cartels might have to take precedence over financial stabilization. They also realized that a general consensus in principle on such issues was all that could be expected. If all principal powers were to join in such a consensus, however, such an outcome would be viewed as contribution enough for one conference. As the report of the preparatory committee noted, "the Committee has borne in mind throughout, that the economic conference must be regarded not as an isolated event but as a stage in the continuous work of international collaboration in the economic sphere which had begun before the project of a general conference was launched and will continue when the conference itself is over" (McClure, 1933, p. 222).

The International Economic Conference was finally held in Geneva in May of 1927. One hundred and ninety-four official delegates and 157 expert advisers attended. Forty-six members of the League were represented, as were the United States, the Soviet Union, and a few other nonmembers. A plethora of resolutions came out of the conference, nearly all of them unanimous. That unanimity was purchased at the cost of specificity and in the absence of binding conviction. Two examples will suffice.

On the thorniest trade issue, the final resolutions reported agreement that the mutual granting of most-favored-nation treatment with respect to customs duties and other conditions of trade was "essential" to the expansion of international trade. Beyond reference to the dangers of exchange-rate depreciation, however, the connection between most-favored-nation treatment and stable finance was not the subject of much discussion. It is true that a number of countries, led by Britain in 1925, had returned to a variant of the gold standard, but many had not.

On the issue of industrial cartels, the conference unanimously recognized the benefits of "rationalization," which, if "coordinated and far reaching," should result in a "better distribution of wealth." Nevertheless, the extent to which "international industrial agreements" contributed to that rationalization could not be specified at the level of principle. National legislation should not necessarily be prejudiced against such "cartels," because they might indeed be "actuated by a sense of the general interest." Recognizing, moreover, that national approaches in fact differed quite strikingly, "effort toward international supervision seemed premature."

18

In light of what was to follow in international economic history, such words leave a bitter taste today. To some extent, they did so even then. One delegate to the conference noted that the resolutions provided nothing more than a "glimpse into the obvious" (McClure, 1933, p. 231). To others, however, the consensus achieved in Geneva was seen as a formidable achievement. On financial as well as trade issues, "a comprehensive code of policy behavior" had been agreed upon (Salter, 1961, pp. 198–199). Conference participants, moreover, designated the League as the institution to flesh out that code and its implications. They even took steps to improve its "machinery" for joint discussion and problem solving.

In practice, this meant that a strengthened secretariat was asked to build on its preparatory work for the conference. The statistical and analytical agenda that would expand throughout the final nineteen years of the League's life had its start at this time, and the organization that pursued that agenda would gradually evolve into a recognizable precursor to the IMF as it would later pursue its mandate for multilateral surveillance. Among its initial tasks after Genoa, the secretariat assisted the Financial Committee of the League in designing new forms of financial aid for troubled countries and new measures to improve the functioning of the gold-exchange standard as it was developing after 1925.

By 1927, the fundamental nature of the League's economic-oversight role had already been defined and delimited both through the results of conferences and through specific lessons learned during technical-assistance missions. The League was to be a seeker of consensus, a reinforcer of natural policy convergence across coequal member states. At most, the League would provide temporary buffers between its members and between members and markets. The markets—in goods, capital, and even in policies—would do the real work through their automatic operations. As we shall see, the unanimity rule and what might be called the "automaticity principle" proved to be fatal flaws in the design of the League's economic machinery. Not coincidentally, both would be eschewed by the architects of the IMF many years later when they recovered and embellished the oversight role the League had pioneered.

Most of the practical tasks assigned to the League in the wake of the Geneva Conference focused directly on the external aspects of policy. Where serious domestic differences existed on issues such as the supervision of cartels, however—differences that might have clear external consequences—League oversight proved to be quite reticent.

19

This makes it all the more ironic that the global economic conflagration that began two years after the Geneva Conference found its spark in the one major area of policy on which the League had the least reticence and the longest history of principled oversight. Despite the apparently durable and practical consensus on first principles of "sound" finance—a consensus that dated back to 1920 in Brussels—the catastrophe began in the financial markets.

The ultimate causes of the Great Depression continue to be much analyzed and much debated (Temin, 1989). This is not the place to rehearse the debate, but it is very much the place to stress an important correlation. When the economic recovery of the 1920s ended, the incipient surveillance machinery of the League became increasingly analytical and decreasingly practical. Encouraging constructive, problem-solving dialogue between competitive states is difficult in the best of times, and the world was now entering the worst of times.

After the Geneva Conference, League staffers envisaged a workable compromise between the restoration of a global "laissez-faire" economic system and the joint political management of the world "as an indivisible economic unit." Per Jacobsson, who would later become managing director of the IMF, was then a member of the League's secretariat. As he saw it:

> [The Geneva Conference] reached a synthesis of the two main economic ideas of the last century expressed, on the one hand, by the Manchester School concentrating upon the advantages of free competition and, on the other hand, by manifold movements aiming at improvement in social conditions and insisting upon the rights of society as a whole (Jacobsson, 1927, p. 53).

Any such synthesis soon unraveled, not at the level of principle, but at the level of practice. Soon after Geneva, those countries that had restored a fixed link between their currencies and gold found themselves with few alternatives to contracting their domestic economies in the face of widening external payments imbalances (Eichengreen, 1992; Simmons, 1994). Business investment, the fuel for economic prosperity, required efficient capital markets. Investment and efficient markets required confidence. Confidence required sound money. And sound money appeared to require both balanced budgets and the anchor of gold convertibility at fixed exchange rates. The unfortunate consequences of policies based on that dominant set of ideas—unemployment and illiquidity—would, statesmen, League officials, and leading economists all hoped, heal themselves. All that was needed was time and fortitude.

Inside the League, agreement on the basic principles, not of Geneva, but of Brussels and Genoa, remained intact and unquestioned until idiosyncratic voices from outside began calling for reconsideration. In hindsight, it might seem that unemployment, which in the United States had climbed from 3 percent in 1929 to 25 percent in 1933, might have created a climate for radical policy change. But the theoretical case for alternative policies had not yet been made, and the real architects of the coming policy revolution, Adolf Hitler and Franklin Roosevelt, were just coming to power. As the last of the great international economic conferences before World War II would show, the case for orthodoxy remained intact.

Liberal Multilateralism in Retreat: The 1930s

Outside the auspices of the League, the famous Dawes and Young Plans, which channeled financial flows from the United States to Germany, rekindled broader international lending for a brief time. The conventional wisdom held that the twin issues of reparations and inter-Allied debt repayments were thereby being resolved. The financial collapse of 1929–31, however, brought these matters back to the fore. In 1932, representatives of the major governments met in Lausanne to negotiate a final settlement. They cancelled remaining reparations payments, although they realized that doing so amounted to launching a very small life raft in a stormy sea. What was to be done to calm the sea itself? Why, call for another conference, of course, and give it a broader mandate. Thus was born the ill-starred World Economic Conference of 1933.

League officials later tried to distance themselves from what many thought must become a debacle. Although no League committee or member of the secretariat recommended the conference, it was technically convoked by a resolution of the League's council. Moreover, the EFO assisted the preparatory committee of experts appointed by Belgium, France, Germany, Italy, Japan, and the United Kingdom. The resulting agenda included a detailed program of action, which demonstrated that the orthodox economic principles of Brussels and Genoa were still dominant.

On monetary issues, the program for London was based on a report approved by officials comprising the Financial Committee of the League (League of Nations, 1932), with one striking exception. The program called for a restoration of the gold-exchange standard, which Britain had once again abandoned in 1931 in the wake of a massive speculative attack on the pound sterling (Kunz, 1987). In order to ensure that countries had adequate gold reserves to enable such a restoration, the program specified that intergovernmental debts must be settled and free international movement of "goods, services, and capital," must be attained. The program predictably advocated that budgets be balanced, but it conceded that somewhat loser monetary policies could stimulate business and help achieve a new equilibrium.

Countries still on the gold-exchange standard were asked to permit the free outward flow of gold and other forms of capital. Countries not on the standard, however, were told not to seek commercial advantage by depreciating the external value of their currencies below the point necessary to reestablish internal equilibrium. Despite the experience of 1931 and the assertion that controls on "unproductive" capital flows might sometimes be justified, the report bluntly urged the abolition of all exchange controls (Helleiner, 1994, pp. 35–36). Central banks were, moreover, to be "independent" and freed from "political interference." They were also to be encouraged to maintain "close and continuous" cooperation with one another. With regard to trade, the program recommended that tariffs should first be frozen at existing levels, then reduced through unilateral, bilateral, and group measures under a multilateral umbrella. Once "normal conditions" returned, unconditional most-favored-nation treatment should form the basis of international commercial relations. Finally, the program urged governments to render their economies more "flexible" (McClure, 1933, pp. 235–239.)

In light of developments then transpiring inside major economies, this blind faith in market solutions in the runup to the 1933 conference is truly breathtaking. The conference program left entirely unspecified any financial or economic role for multilateral institutions such as the League. The consequence of that silence, which would have been reinforced by the secondary role played by the League secretariat in the preparations, seems clear. Any future League oversight function would be limited to clarifying the rationale for orthodox policies based on enlightened self-interest. Rightly conceived at the level of principle, national policies aimed at restoring a functioning gold-exchange standard without capital controls and creating a transparent and free trading system would automatically achieve optimal internal and external equilibria. Impeccable ideas rule, once they are explained clearly enough!

In fact, government policies around the world were moving in precisely the opposite direction. The problem was not that conditions had become inauspicious for collective action along the road of established

22

principles. It was that the principles themselves were being discredited by experience even as the London Conference was called to order. The most "flexible" national economy was then watching its banking system collapse. The "sound-money" policies of the U.S. Federal Reserve were just then deepening a major liquidity crisis and sapping business confidence. In such an environment, the United States left the gold-exchange standard just before the conference opened. Shaped by ortho-dox fears of inflationary spirals, balanced budgets were accelerating deflation in the United States and elsewhere. In Germany, orthodox fiscal policy had just helped snuff the life out of a comatose Weimar Republic. The constituency for liberal commercial policies was in full retreat around the world. Competitive currency depreciation had become commonplace.[26]

When the World Economic Conference finally convened in London in June 1933, the spokesmen for the sixty-six nations represented still could not bring themselves to depart from orthodoxy. Nevertheless, the cognitive dissonance created by the widening gap between economic theory and actual policy stimulated a deepening debate both within and beyond the secretariat of the League. The broader debate continues to this day, and it would be fruitless to attempt a summation here. Suffice it to note that in the 1930s, despite lengthening odds against ortho-doxy, the orthodox position retained its intellectual respectability.

Friedrich von Hayek, the famous Austrian economist, then at the London School of Economics, built an impressive edifice of theory suggesting that market-interventionist policies typically did more harm than good in the long run. He was certainly not alone. Keynes and his allies picked up the cudgels on precisely this point, albeit from a conviction that deep depressions bred unusual circumstances. The theoretical revolution thereby sparked seems clear to us now, but in 1933, its core ideas were not yet fully formulated or compelling. With no lodestar other that the principles of Brussels and Genoa to guide them, the delegates to the London Conference thus had no basis for recommending new departures in national economic policies. Imagine their consternation, then, when their collective appeal to the United States for leadership in restoring the gold-exchange standard (after an orderly devaluation and realignment of exchange rates) brought a blunt and personal rejection from President Roosevelt himself. For good

[26] The debate continues over the actual effects of such exchange-rate policies and on the incentives for and consequences of cheating on agreed upon monetary arrangements (Eichengreen and Sachs, 1985; Rogoff, 1985; Oye, 1992; Eichengreen, 1995).

measure, the president excoriated "the fetishes of so-called international bankers" (U.S. Department of State, 1933, pp. 673–674; Skidelsky, 1992, p. 481).[27]

In July 1933, the World Economic Conference dissolved in intellectual and political disarray. As Keynes wrote at the time, there was "no cat in the bag, no rabbits in the hat, no brains in the head." Its consequence was "miserable confusion and unutterable waste of opportunity" brought about by "an obstinate adherence to ancient rules of thumb." More tellingly and less self-servingly, Keynes concluded that new rules of thumb or even common sense could promise no better outcome. New rules would matter only if "a single power or a like-minded group of powers" could forge a new and practical consensus upon them (Skidelsky, 1992, p. 482).[28]

To Keynes, as well as to many of his contemporaries, the weak link in the system, as it had evolved quite incrementally throughout the 1920s, was finance. As noted, a quite robust consensus emerged after the Armistice that private financial markets should be relied upon to support economic reconstruction and expansion. The mobility of private capital internationally, stable exchange rates promised by a restored gold-exchange standard, and national monetary autonomy formed a coherent whole. It remains difficult to imagine what other combination of policies could have been more practicable in the circumstances of the 1920s. That the consequence of following these policies was a speculative financial boom ending in profound economic collapse is clear only in hindsight.

Financiers then as now repeat the mantra "sound money, sound policies," because they know their activities depend upon stable expectations of value, risk, and repayment. After the unanimity of the 1927 conference, it seemed to everyone that a principled basis for stable expectations had been restored. But practice did not follow principles, and iconoclasts such as Keynes were only beginning to think that the problem lay in the principles themselves. The economic arm of the

[27] On the underexamined domestic political roots of Roosevelt's position, see Eichengreen and Uzan, 1993.

[28] A vast literature has developed on such themes, some of it focusing specifically on the 1933 conference. John Odell (1988), for example, compares the bargaining strategies employed then with the Bretton Woods experience. He concludes that a given structure of international power may preclude certain extreme outcomes but still permit a wide set of outcomes. To explain the precise outcome of 1933, he underlines the importance of large swings in national market conditions, painful national experience that discredits prevailing policy ideas, and international technical disagreement.

League, which was itself bound up in the articulation of those principles, was caught in the contradiction. As Salter (1961, pp. 196–197) recalled, with a characteristic and far-from-disinterested degree of overstatement:

> Everything which was begun [by the League] early enough to come to fruition in the twenties was successful; everything that could not reach this stage till the thirties failed. Thus the plans which the Financial Committee were considering after their earlier work had been completed (whether on financial assistance in a new form to other countries in difficulty or the victims of aggression or on reform of the gold standard), all came to nothing. Unhappily, the same fate . . . befell the major task attempted by the economic section—the establishment of a better foundation of commercial policy for international trade.[29]

In the mid to late 1930s, however, the ultimate futility of the League's work could only be sensed. All hopes were not yet dashed, and the work continued. As the terrible decade advanced, the operational side of the League's oversight role fell into disuse. Its analytical side, however, was just coming to the fore. That shift in emphasis did not stop the depression or impede preparations for war, but it did shape the worldviews of individuals who would bridge the distance between the League and the IMF in their own careers.

Analytical Oversight During the Great Depression

Despite the sense of foreboding that enveloped the economic work of the League after 1933, a quite remarkable transformation began to occur inside the organization. The constructive consequences of that transformation would, ironically, become evident only after the League itself ceased to exist. Forged in the cauldron of the 1930s, a new model, a new procedure, and a new pragmatism quietly reshaped the practice of multilateral economic oversight in the final decade of the League's existence. Forced by hard political facts to retreat from the more assertive role that marked their predecessors in the 1920s, a retreat reinforced by the political dynamics of international economic negotiations during the war years, the EFO became a central analytical

[29] It is interesting to note that after Salter retired from the directorship of the EFO in 1931, he returned to government work in Britain and fell into the emerging Keynesian circle. On the great internal debate over unbalancing the government's budget, he apparently sided with Keynes as early as 1933. One of the great principles of League orthodoxy was evidently proving itself to be quite fragile, although in this case, the British government itself continued to adhere to orthodox prescriptions (Skidelsky, 1992, pp. 467–468).

apparatus for shaping a new policy consensus. In this respect, it became, by accident and not by design, a direct precursor to the contemporary IMF.

To be sure, less esoteric work continued at the League during the early to mid-1930s. The financial panic that swept Europe after 1931 devastated the countries whose external borrowing the League had supervised in the 1920s. Austria, Hungary, and others were quickly pushed from hard-won solvency back to the brink of default. When they appealed once more for League assistance, methods applied before were applied again. League representatives calmed international lenders, helped craft new syndicates (often under official guarantees from leading European governments), and directly supervised debt-servicing operations in borrowing countries. Once again, this most concrete manifestation of multilateral oversight, although concentrated on less politically sensitive cases and of marginal importance when all of Europe was heading toward the abyss of total war, was a harbinger of things to come many decades later when the IMF would play a similar role (Eichengreen and Lindert, 1989). The abysmal failure of the London Conference, however, could not help but affect the way in which the League approached its less visible economic and financial tasks.

The high-water mark for the League's earlier approach to systemic oversight had, in fact, been reached in 1927. Throughout the 1920s, the chief objective of the League had been to frame international conventions "to facilitate economic and financial relations between nations and thus contribute towards fulfilling the economic obligations laid upon members of the League by the Covenant" (Hill, 1945, p. 71). On the basis of "international legislation" at the level of principle, markets would work much as they had in the era before World War I. Only a few agreed upon rules were necessary, most importantly, the rules of the gold-exchange standard and of nondiscriminatory trade. Any adjustments that were needed in other domestic policies or arrangements so as to facilitate peaceful international intercourse would occur automatically if the basic rules were honored.

After 1933, such a stance became increasingly untenable. The League therefore adapted its oversight role in two ways. First, although it never attempted to convene another world economic conference, the League did gather information, draft reports, and sponsor meetings on specific questions, such as the trade-depressing issue of double taxation. When such meetings occurred, however, the League always limited attendees to those states most directly involved, and it often sought to promote bilateral "model" agreements that might over time become multilateralized. Second, the League devoted an increasing amount of attention to systemic analysis, much of which pointed to the need for governments and international agencies deliberately to encourage convergent domestic policies. In short, the deficiency of markets left to their own devices became the focal point for the League's analytical work. Research concentrated increasingly on the underlying conditions necessary to foster the kinds of convergence in national economic policies deemed necessary for the effective operation of sound markets.

Alexander Loveday, director of the EFO from 1931 until the end, likened the most obvious application of the latter method of operation to the establishment of special governmental commissions or inquiries, a method that continues to be quite common in parliamentary systems throughout the world (Loveday, 1938). Commissions can, indeed, be useful tools of government—sometimes to build a constituency for a specific policy change through studies and consultations and sometimes to postpone change until such a constituency emerges. So it was in the 1930s, when the League created expert committees to address such matters as multilateral payments systems, exchange controls, restrictions on the sale of raw materials, and standards for international loan contracts. As the decade wore on, the issues broadened to cover the full range of macroeconomic policies that lay behind the depression.

The League's new approach built on the precedent of its first survey compiled in 1922 at the behest of the Brussels Conference. As a method of systemic oversight, it seemed a natural outgrowth of the kinds of preparatory work the staff had always done before major conferences. Data was collected by neutral observers, general patterns were identified, and recommendations were made. The real novelty of the approach lay in the framing of those recommendations in terms of the facts as League analysts perceived them rather than in terms of orthodox economic principles.

Within the secretariat of the League, staff members had been assigned the task of gathering, analyzing, and publishing economic statistics as early as 1919. Over time, an Economic Intelligence Service (EIS) was formally organized within the Economic, Financial, and Transit Department. By the 1930s, the EIS had developed into a kind of internal think tank, although it was still modest in scale. Aside from regular statistical publications—the direct ancestors of contemporary statistical series published by the IMF and other international economic agencies—the service also published an annual volume entitled, *World Economic Survey*. It was written largely by prominent consultants to the

League, J. B. Condliffe in the early 1930s, and James Meade from 1938 to 1940. Its descendant is the IMF's *World Economic Outlook*, which the IMF describes as a central element in the contemporary practice of multilateral economic surveillance.[30]

In addition to Condliffe and Meade, a remarkable group of economists came to be associated with the League's EIS, either directly as staff members and overseers or indirectly as consultants. These included Gottfried Haberler, Alvin Hansen, Folke Hilgerdt, Tjalling Koopmans, Ragnar Nurkse, Jan Tinbergen, J. M. Fleming, Jacques Polak, and Louis Rasminsky (de Marchi, 1991; Polak, 1995a, 1995b). All would later influence the work of the IMF, and the last three would rise to prominence in the ranks of its senior staff and on its executive board.

In 1933, the Rockefeller Foundation began supplementing the resources devoted by the League to the EIS. Driven by concern over the deepening consequences of the depression, the foundation's purpose in providing an annual grant of $125,000 was to stimulate a broad research program on the international transmission of business cycles.[31] Most notably, the grant helped support a seminal study by Haberler, first published by the League in 1937.[32] Tinbergen and Polak then completed a massive empirical study aimed at testing Haberler's central hypotheses. With the publication of Tinbergen's two-volume *Statistical Testing of Business Cycle Theories* (1939a, 1939b) and follow-up work by Koopmans, Meade, and Nurkse, the EIS pioneered the field of open-economy macroeconomics. The theoretical and methodological underpinnings for multilateral economic surveillance as today practiced by the IMF and other international institutions may be traced back to that work and to a series of policy-oriented studies undertaken by the EIS during the war.

As the political situation in Europe was deteriorating and war seemed imminent, League officials sought to build on their analytical

[30] As Polak points out, there is an important difference between the two publications. The *Survey* was addressed to the world at large, and it was hortatory. The *World Economic Outlook* is meant to be a policy document that guides the authoritative organs of the IMF, its executive board and interim and development committees, and provides the broad framework for a full range of related policy debates (personal correspondence, April 21, 1995).

[31] The Rockefeller Foundation also provided the League with $50,000 for the study of the double-taxation issue mentioned above (de Marchi, 1991, p. 153–155).

[32] The volume was subsequently revised twice, mainly to take account of Keynes' *The General Theory of Employment, Interest, and Money* (1936) and other work stimulated by Keynes' study. The final League version appeared as Haberler's *Prosperity and Depression* (1941).

28

work by presenting governments with an accessible compilation of advice on countercyclical economic policies. A "Special Delegation on Depressions" was established and asked to undertake the task. The delegation actually comprised an eight-member subcommittee of the Economic and Financial Committees of the League. Two members were appointed from each committee, one was seconded from the International Labor Organization, and three outside experts were engaged—Oskar Morgenstern, Jacques Rueff, and Bertil Ohlin. The composition of the delegation changed somewhat during the war years. Throughout its work, however, it was assisted by Loveday and his staff, including Nurkse, Polak, and Rasminsky.[33] Three major publications resulted: *The Transition from War to Peace Economy* (League of Nations, 1943); *International Currency Experience* (Nurkse, 1944); and *Economic Stability in the Post-War World* (League of Nations, 1945).[34]

The studies of the delegation were widely acknowledged as having a significant impact on policymaking, both during and after the war. They did not, of course, appear in a vacuum, and the intellectual consensus they articulated needs to be interpreted in the context of the gathering Keynesian revolution. Moreover, they would be criticized immediately after the war for exaggerating the risk of a reversion to depression and for not giving sufficient attention to the problem of latent inflation (Black, 1991, p. 58). A few themes bear emphasis, however, for they anticipated the mandates assigned by the victorious powers to a new set of international economic institutions after the war.

The reports underlined the need for "progressive removal of obstructions to trade," avoidance of competitive cycles of currency depreciation, acknowledgment of the "international character of cyclical economic depressions," and "courageous international measures of reconstruction and development" (League of Nations, 1943, p. 14; Polak, 1939). None of these goals, it was noted, could be reached in the absence of more intensive cooperation between states. Throughout the interwar period, this truism lay behind the oft-repeated appeal for states to pursue their "enlightened self-interest" by remolding their national economic policies around the ideals of free trade and the gold standard. The depression studies innovatively grounded that appeal in negotiated codes of

[33] On Rasminsky's role, see Granatstein, 1981, pp. 175–176, and Plumptre, 1977, pp. 39–58, 125–170.

[34] Technically, the first and third were linked as parts I and II of the Report of the Delegation. Providing background for this work, the Fiscal Committee of the League (League of Nations, 1939) published an analysis of the central debate concerning the advisability or inadvisability of unbalanced budgets during depressionary troughs.

conduct that entailed deliberate efforts to render compatible domestic policies that had external effects. Gone was the earlier faith in the efficacy of markets guided by vague commitments to nondiscriminatory trade and currency stability.

Loveday, who directed the League's depression reports and personally contributed to the first, claimed to have come to just such a conclusion as early as 1937 (de Marchi, p. 177).[35] Moreover, for such codes to be more than the idealistic expressions of principle that the League's economic pronouncements had been since the Brussels Conference, Loveday asserted that they required monitors and arbiters with real authority. Loveday's thinking anticipated the surveillance mandate of the IMF as it would later evolve, although the extent of the IMF's actual authority would fall short of his vision.[36]

In a more direct way, the reports also pushed the incipient new consensus, which we now identify with Keynes' *General Theory* (1936), beyond the old mantra of free trade and the gold standard. As might have been expected in the midst of a war that pitted democratic systems of government against totalitarian ones, the first report stressed the "liberty of each individual" to make basic economic choices. But such liberty could only be meaningful and contribute to "rising standards of living" in all countries when governments provided the necessary domestic conditions to ensure that "no man or woman able and willing to work should be unable to obtain employment for periods of time longer than is needed to transfer from one occupation to another or, when necessary, to acquire a new skill" (League of Nations, 1943, p. 14). For such full-employment policies to work worldwide without compromising the overarching goals of expanded trade and stable exchange rates, the ultimate conclusion of the earlier studies of Haberler and Tinbergen seemed unavoidable. Relevant *national* policies, including broad and politically sensitive macroeconomic policies, must be coordinated directly by the states themselves, if necessary through intermediary agencies created by them for just such a purpose. No external constraint, no autonomous market, nothing beyond their own political will could bring those policies to converge in the cause of global

[35] De Marchi, who convincingly develops this theme, notes that the idea was also explicit in the work of other League economists, such as Condliffe. Business-cycle studies by Haberler Tinbergen, and Polak moved in the same direction.

[36] By 1942, Keynes had worked out a concrete proposal along these lines for an international clearing union. The union was to be founded on a code of conduct centered on nondiscrimination, convertibility, and symmetry in adjustment obligations between surplus and deficit countries.

economic stability and enduring prosperity. The underlying logic reversed the old orthodoxy. Coordinated policies could not be guaranteed by allowing markets to function almost without restraint, on the basis of minimal rules and supposedly consensual principles; properly functioning markets themselves depended upon deliberately coordinated policies.

It is significant that the League's depression reports emphasized trade in "raw materials and manufactured goods," rather than international flows of capital. Even though Nurkse's *International Currency Experience* (1944) laid substantial blame for interwar economic disorder on speculative capital flows, the reports did not embrace the idea of capital controls in principle. Indeed, capital flows were a vital component of the early world-system models of Tinbergen and Polak, which lay in the background. Moreover, there was no bias in these studies against what would later be called "equilibrating capital flows." But there was also no answer to the question of how to differentiate such flows in practice from disequilibrating flows, a question that would later plague the Bretton Woods System.

The depression reports presumed that financial flows to accommodate expanding trade would be important for the avoidance of depressions after the war, and they did not envisage the continuation of the extensive system of capital controls that had been built up during the conflict. Nevertheless, without being completely explicit, they did envisage a postwar system that would give priority to trade and therefore to exchange-rate stability, rather than to international capital mobility.[37] The freedom of capital movements, although desirable, would have to be conditional, especially in a context in which governments would pursue activist employment policies while avoiding competitive currency depreciation and other "obstructions to trade." But on what would they be conditional? The League reports, once again, provided the answer: such freedom should be conditional on effective arrangements for international coordination of a full range of national economic policies affecting exchange rates.

The final economic studies of the League contributed to a new consensus that ultimately found its authoritative expression in the 1944 Bretton Woods Agreement and in the 1947 Havana Charter. In short,

[37] Such a trade-off can usefully be understood in terms of now-standard foundations of open-economy macroeconomics; see, for example, Kenen, 1994, chaps. 14–15. On the political implications of what has come to be known as the Mundell-Fleming model, see Cohen, 1993.

the studies helped provide the intellectual basis for rejecting the governing principles and methods that came out of the Brussels and Genoa Conferences. In terms of our own contemporary debates, the earlier consensus rested on four planks: free trade, exchange-rate stability, balanced budgets, and capital mobility. The new consensus promoted "the progressive removal of obstructions to trade," "orderly" exchange-rate adjustment (either up or down as warranted by internal and external economic fundamentals) through a transparent set of monitored arrangements, countercyclical fiscal and monetary policies, and capital mobility to the extent necessary to facilitate those prior objectives.

The old policy consensus informed the two-dimensional multilateral oversight function of the League: it provided principles for direct application in financially desperate countries, and it oriented pioneering analytical surveys of the international economy. The new consensus shaped the incipient surveillance functions of the international agencies that rose from the ashes of the League. As would become clear over time, especially in the case of the IMF, those functions would now have three dimensions. The first two were similar in form to those of the League. The third reflected the nature of the intergovernmental codes of conduct crafted at the start of an era of activist economic policies. Whereas the principled oversight of the League promised but rarely delivered "automatic" adjustments to the pressures of openness, the surveillance operations of the IMF eventually applied few rules and many flexible policy guidelines to all member states on a case-by-case basis. Over time, those operations moved far beyond the immediate postwar goal of removing exchange restrictions to encompass the range of national economic policies having external effects. Throughout the course of its evolution, however, IMF surveillance left considerably more room for judgment and political accommodation than the principles of Brussels and Genoa had ever allowed. Although such flexibility would often prove frustrating to economic purists, a basic pragmatism was built into the organization of the IMF from the beginning.

The IMF was to provide an institutional buffer for states now seeking both national economic security and international economic prosperity (Ruggie, 1982, 1991, 1994). Bitter experience in the 1930s suggested that markets that were beyond national control threatened economic security, and the war convinced many that economic closure could never guarantee prosperity. Freer trade, a stable exchange-rate system, regulated capital markets, and coordinated macroeconomic policies comprised core elements of a new approach to international

32

economic governance. The IMF and other multilateral institutions were to help manage the tricky politics this approach entailed. That would sometimes mean serving as the scapegoat for unpopular policies within member states. More important, at the systemic level, it meant working to foster common understandings of collective problems and being available for crisis management when breakdown threatened. In this new world, markets were no longer ends in themselves. Rather, they provided a useful means to a political end.

In the Shadow of the League

The League was well represented at the 1944 Bretton Woods Conference. Loveday attended as an official observer. Polak, having left the League in 1943, was a member of the Dutch delegation. Rasminsky, who also left the League in 1943 to become an official in the Canadian government, attended and played a key role in brokering the main negotiations between the Americans and the British. There exists very little evidence, however, that the chief architects of the new system drew seriously or directly on the League's experience. Neither Polak nor Rasminsky recall Loveday having any real impact on the proceedings (personal interviews: Rasminsky, August 11, 1993; Polak, September 19, 1994). Their own thinking was, of course, shaped by their years at the League, but both concede that the British, and especially the Americans, spent little time thinking about what had gone before. The League-sponsored business cycle and depression studies were in the background, of course, but so was Keynes' *General Theory*, in the person of Keynes himself. Nevertheless, the bright lights of Keynes' ideas, the extent of America's power in the Bretton Woods era, and the obscurity of the interwar experience may have blinded us to the enduring impact of the League on the IMF as it evolved in later years.

As Martin Hill explained when the EFO was closing:

> The creation of the Organization represented an entirely new departure in peacetime interstate relationships. . . . Numerous multilateral agreements that would not have been possible without an appropriate international machinery were concluded. . . . Consultation between officials engaged in framing and executing economic and social policies in different countries was rare before 1914; through the League it became an established practice. Even more important perhaps was the remarkable change in general public attitudes toward international consideration of economic problems. . . . In 1920, national tariffs were generally held to be a matter of purely domestic concern. The same is true of many other problems, the interna-

33

tional consideration of which is now just as generally considered to be normal and desirable (Hill, 1945, pp. 3–4).

Similar statements would be made about the IMF years later, but we need to ask whether such a view of the League, in retrospect, warrants skepticism.

Certainly, Lord Salter, the first permanent director of the EFO, thought so when he published his memoirs in 1961. Despite the achievements of the League, Salter focused, as have most commentators since then, on the League's ultimate failure, which he blamed on "the intrinsic weakness of an 'inter-state' institution: a deterioration in the relations between its principal members can quickly reduce it to impotence." To Salter, the League represented merely "organized diplomacy, not an organ of Government. . . [and] it is an illusion to believe that 'technical' work of real importance can continue successfully if there is a basic disunity in the controlling political authority" (Salter, 1961, pp. 200–201). The shock of war, more than any institutional creation of states, accounted for whatever cooperative impulses came to characterize the contemporary period.

But Salter's realism is more problematic than Hill's idealism. The kind of supranational institution conjured by the image of a unified "controlling political authority" is unimaginable in any world with an international political structure resembling our own. Equally unimaginable is the autonomous work of "technical" organizations in such a context. The history surveyed in this essay supports a more complex view of the League and its legacy.

The economic work of the League was neither irrelevant to the period after World War II nor was it forgotten. In a number of important respects, the experience foreshadowed what would come later. Lessons learned over the course of the League's existence, moreover, were transmitted directly into at least one of its most important postwar analogues.

In the 1920s, the restoration of a world economy on the foundation of global financial markets seemed to require a basic form of collaboration among states. In institutional terms, they needed a buffer. The League's halting and often frustrating engagement in the incipient practice of systemic oversight developed in this environment. In its directly applied form, that is, in response to Central European debt crises, that role was straightforward. States principally needed an institution to blame for anticipated failure, but they also welcomed the slight chance that the coordinating function provided by that institution could avoid such failure. In its more analytical form, and in an age of conference diplomacy, states needed the instrumentality of League oversight to compile reliable data across different national settings, to diagnose trends, and to suggest directions for mutually beneficial policy adjustments.

Both forms of oversight were practiced in the 1920s, and both relied upon a fairly general consensus among League members on economic principles that applied equally to all. By the late 1920s, after many conferences, such a consensus existed. The principles of the gold standard, fiscal conservatism, and nondiscriminatory trade, as well as the belief that any necessary policy adjustments would come automatically once agreement on such principles had been reached, had become an ideology—useful for keeping capital flowing, at least for a time, but increasingly out of step with the real world inside national political economies. The principled consensus thus proved to be theoretical at best and illusory at worst.

The 1930s transformed the oversight role of the League and privileged its analytical face.[38] The economic catastrophe of that decade also overthrew the earlier ideology and dramatically promoted the virtues of pragmatism. It did not, however, subvert the idea that a multilateral buffer would be needed if a world characterized by decentralized political authority were to return to the path of economic and financial integration. As in the 1920s, that buffer was there to provide crisis management as well as a target for blame in the event of failure. The organization's analytical role, however, differed from that of the 1920s. The League would still compile and assess cross-national data; it would still organize conferences, albeit more focused and less ambitious ones; and it would still make suggestions for sound national policies. But its overarching goal would be to facilitate deliberate policy coordination. In a world chary of rules that no power could render binding, the League tried to provide the rationale for discretionary national policies to move in internationally constructive directions.

The ambition behind such systemic oversight, and the hard experience that shaped it, was transmitted from a dying League to a rising IMF. The negotiations at Bretton Woods and, even more clearly, those that at Savannah in 1946 actually activated the IMF, put an end to the dream of automaticity. National policies having external economic effects would have to be supervised and adjusted—if necessary, through

[38] Something similar happened at the Bank for International Settlements. Pushed to the political margins shortly after its establishment in 1929, its staff produced a number of useful studies on longer-term issues during the 1930s (Schloss, 1958).

political coordination facilitated by an intermediary. The initial focus of that coordination, and, thus, of the intermediary's mandate, was on exchange rates and exchange restrictions. Over time, and as the exchange-rate system became even more discretionary, the lens widened and the mandate became more expansive.

Precisely how was the experience of the League transmitted to the IMF? Keynes' famous thesis about the unacknowledged influence of economic ideas on practical men has long suggested important links in such cases. Failed ideas associated with the early League were swamped by the 1930s. In reaction, the Great Depression and World War II shaped a new heterodoxy. The painful lessons learned by the League seemed simply to be in the air when the IMF began its institutional journey.

Recent applied research on the influence of ideas within the field of international relations suggests something similar. Neofunctionalists, for example, cite the emergence of specialized networks that facilitate the international transmission of ideas relevant to policy. In consequence of interaction within such networks, mandates for technical, problem-solving organizations can more or less rationally be formulated (Ruggie, 1975; Haas, 1980). In such a view, the IMF, and the League before it, reflect functional necessities, and any similarities between the two organizations arise from similarities in broader circumstances as perceived by relevant elites or from the lessons of failed experiments as commonly understood.

Not far afield, students of "epistemic communities" underline the emergence of "politically relevant collective understandings of the physical and social world that are subject to political selection processes and thus to evolutionary change" (Adler and Haas, 1992, p. 372). Practically speaking, that selection—or social learning—takes the form of a generalized process of socialization among elites (Ikenberry and Kupchan, 1990). In such a context, the experience of the League was simply one among a number of historical factors shaping the worldview of elites who, in turn, influenced the Fund's development.

Clearly, these approaches are plausible, and they help to draw indirect linkages between the League and the IMF. But the historical material surveyed in this essay suggests a much more direct connection. It suggests, in short, that social learning requires teachers. For short periods of time, Jacobsson, Fleming, and Rasminsky brought the lessons they had learned in the League straight into the IMF. Jacobsson, in particular, did so quite consciously and was only too willing to share his reflections on the League and on the constraints under which it labored (Pauly, 1992, p. 309). The most significant link, however, is Polak.

Polak left the League in 1943, after seven years on the staff. In 1947, he joined the IMF. After helping to establish the Fund's statistical operations, he moved to the research department, where he was to be its guiding spirit throughout the next thirty years. During much that period, it was widely recognized both inside and outside the IMF that the two key members of the Fund's staff were Jacques Polak and Joseph Gold of the legal department. After retiring from the staff in 1979, Polak served on the executive board of the IMF until 1986. Since then, he has retained an office in the headquarters building, carried on with his own research, and served in an informal advisory capacity. Gold has done the same.

In 1991, a festschrift in honor of Jacques Polak (Frenkel and Goldstein, 1991) hailed his achievements and traced his contributions to the manner and methods by which the IMF has pursued its principal roles throughout the postwar period. Although the League years are mentioned in passing, the emphasis is more contemporary. Summarizing a vast body of pioneering research, the introduction recounts the lessons Polak has taught generations of Fund economists.[39]

Economic analysis should start with the facts as they can be ascertained, and it should be policy oriented. Analysis is not enough, however, because policymakers need practical tools with which to achieve concrete goals. Exchange-rate adjustment should be seen as a useful, even at times essential, tool for achieving internal and external balance in national economies. And in a world of decentralized political authority, disciplined monetary and fiscal policies must precede exchange-rate stability. Given the existence of spillovers across interdependent national economies, moreover, information sharing, at least, and policy coordination, at best, can stabilize the world economy. Economists must understand, however, the depth of domestic political constraints on joint policymaking at the international level. In view of those constraints, policy coordination will be most successful when spillover effects are most obvious, when external obligations and agreed upon rules of conduct are specific and not moralistic in nature, and when compliance can be readily monitored (Gold, 1988). Intermediaries such as the IMF have proven useful in such circumstances, but large-scale conferences and other forms of centralized decisionmaking have not. The onus must remain on individual countries to adjust their economies as needed to achieve stable growth.

---

[39] A festschrift honoring Gold two years earlier (Norton, 1989) notes Gold's similarly seminal contributions to the field of international monetary law.

Polak's students point to three subthemes underlying these lessons: the importance of pragmatism, a preference for induction over deduction, and the need for skepticism regarding policy prescriptions based on simple economic principles. These subthemes are, in fact, a distillation of the hard lessons learned by the staff of the League. They flow directly from the historical experience surveyed above, but they did not flow directly into the experience of the IMF. During the early years of the Bretton Woods System, the experience of the League was ignored. Its lessons had to be recovered and reapplied. In short, they had to be taught.

The literature on policy networks and epistemic communities provides few examples of the way in which social learning actually occurs and becomes institutionalized. The history surveyed in this essay, however, suggests that individual teachers can be vitally important in transferring lessons from one institutional context to another.[40] In this regard, an old idea associated with Max Weber is relevant. The staffs of institutions embody collective memory. Weaken those institutions, and societies and their leaders risk forgetting. Ideas do not float freely. Individuals possessing good ideas can have an impact, but most likely under fortunate circumstances that enable them to test those ideas, apply them, and pass them on (Finnemore, 1993).

Individuals working inside the League during the 1920s confronted an opportunity to organize a mechanism for international economic oversight. Universal principles were articulated and then applied in several financially troubled countries. In this limited arena, the League compensated for both capital-market failure and political failure; the restoration of capital flows into Austria and Hungary in the late 1920s were testimony to an unexpected success. But the League was never permitted to extend that oversight to the most politically sensitive debtor countries, such as Poland and Germany.[41] After 1929, neither the League nor the new Bank for International Settlements could compensate or substitute for the absence of stabilizing and adequate capital inflows in these cases. Even more fundamental, the League was

[40] Directly relevant to this point is a well-examined thesis in the field of organization theory that policy entrepreneurs can have an important impact on the shape of institutions and the character of policies when windows of opportunity open (see, for example, Kingdon, 1984; Brooks and Gagnon, 1990, 1994).

[41] I am grateful to Harold James for emphasizing this point in personal correspondence. On the Polish case and the more general phenomenon of states and creditors seeking to resolve debt problems outside the forum of the League, and in general, in *ad hoc* and insufficiently institutionalized settings, see Meyer (1970).

never able to apply its principles in the most powerful states, not only because the most powerful state of all was not a League member but, more important, because those principles themselves were increasingly out of step with political realities within and among those states.

The IMF would also be constrained in its ability to influence powerful states, even though its own multilateral-surveillance mandate would eventually rest on a firmer legal and political foundation. With regard to weaker states, however, it would play a much more prominent role than the League had played. In several instances—notably the generalized crisis that followed Mexico's declaration of a debt-repayment moratorium in 1982 and the more recent attempt to stabilize the transitional economies of Russia and its neighbors—the IMF has served on the front lines as leading states and private creditors have struggled to devise collective responses. A large body of research on the politics of international institutions now speaks to the various issues raised in such a comparison between the League and the IMF (for example, Keohane, 1984, 1989; Ruggie, 1993). This is not the place to attempt a synthesis, but one theme emerges that deserves more research.

The League provided a buffer for several Central European countries in the early 1920s. Acting as more than just an international or domestic scapegoat in the event of likely failure, the League stepped into the breach caused by the fact that the primary objective of all creditor states in those years was to prevent the spread of contagion to their own markets, not to cure the disease at its source. In such circumstances, the limited oversight role of the League was not transformed from nice in principle to essential in practice. It became, quite simply, useful.

That the incipient surveillance function of the League was not entirely abandoned in the 1930s is as interesting as the fact that its analogue in the IMF was raised to prominence only after the original rules of the Bretton Woods exchange-rate system were destroyed in the 1970s. With respect to the most general systemic issues, the mandate of both the League and IMF became more analytical, and in both cases, the pursuit of that mandate helped significantly to reshape the intellectual milieu for the formulation of economic policy. In neither case, however, did leading states demonstrate by their actions that international factors now held sway in their domestic policymaking. Nevertheless, multilateral analysis and systemic oversight in both periods reinforced the emergence of new paradigms concerning the requisites of economic stabilization within states. In both the League and the IMF, moreover, the actual practice of systemic oversight came to emphasize the importance of coordinating the macroeconomic policies pursued within those states.

Beyond such parallels, my personal view is that the experience of the League continues to have a direct, if implied, impact on the IMF and its core mandate. The League, in short, stands in memory as an important negative example. At the very least, its ultimately unhappy experience continues to provide a warning to those who are skeptical of the need for international political institutions in a world of integrating markets—especially integrating capital markets—or who see such institutions simply as glorified think tanks. To the extent that leading states choose to pursue their own national objectives through increasingly linked capital markets, and until they are willing to anchor those markets in durably integrated political structures, the possibility of uncontainable financial crises requires that they maintain an intergovernmental mechanism for preventing or handling emergencies. More broadly, when states exhibit strong preferences for both autonomy in economic policy making and deeper financial integration, they must find ways to manage constructively the symbiotic interaction between exchange rates and international capital flows (Pauly, 1997). The history of the League testifies to the fact that such an objective is immeasurably more difficult to achieve in the absence of an effective institutional intermediary.

In the 1920s, leading states attempted to pursue their own national objectives through restored international capital markets, but they proved unwilling or unable to ground those markets in an enduring gold-exchange standard or any other workable political regime. In such an environment, the failure even to consider transforming the EFO into a reliable crisis manager or to craft a substitute with the requisite degree of political legitimacy soon proved lethal. When, beginning in the 1970s, leading states next attempted to give a central place in the international economic order to international capital markets, the memory of that earlier failure helped shape a new mandate for the IMF. In the 1980s and 1990s, an organization with the legitimacy, resources, and analytical capability for crisis management was therefore available. No single individual was responsible for this, but social learning was reflected in the legal charter of the IMF as well as in the work of certain individuals who imported into the IMF the intellectual tools necessary to play such a role, tools crafted in part by activities that took place in the League even in its darkest period.

I do not mean to imply that the IMF can contribute to the welfare of international society only when financial crises are imminent. The

IMF can and does perform many useful tasks on a daily basis. It has also demonstrated an ability to adapt itself to vastly changed operating environments, an ability occasionally tempered by reticence in questioning new orthodoxies that it has helped foster (Haas, 1990; Kahler, 1995; Clark, 1996). I also do not mean to suggest that only the IMF can help avoid or contain future financial catastrophes. Indeed, we are currently witnessing a proliferation of governmental, central-bank, and private-sector forums for financial-risk management and associated policy collaboration (Kapstein, 1994). Parallels to the 1920s may be disquieting in this regard, but I would not argue that substitutes for the IMF are impossible to envisage. I do mean to suggest, however, that the surveillance functions of international economic organizations such as the IMF address core interests of leading states, not just weak states, and that the prospect of financial crises brings these interests to the fore.

The multilateral economic surveillance pioneered by the League and carried on by the IMF is fundamentally aimed at avoiding financial crises. In both the League and the IMF, however, an evolving mandate for systemic oversight underpinned operational capacities for assisting in the resolution of financial crises when they nevertheless arose. In the case of the League, such a capacity was only beginning to emerge. Worth emphasizing, however, is the observation that it began to erode even when member states still appeared broadly to share a principled consensus on international economic objectives.

Whether crises help or hinder the institutionalization of collaborative international mechanisms in the long run remains a complicated and open question. The experience of the League after 1929 suggests one answer; the experience of the IMF in the 1980s and 1990s suggests another. Other variables are obviously important, but the broad sweep of the League's history in the monetary and financial arena clearly implies that integrated financial markets, through which spillovers occur ever more fluidly across national economies, do not run themselves. It also implies that in an emergency, national authorities operating independently cannot be counted on to save those markets, especially when a consensus on basic principles of economic policy begins to look like an idealogy. Institutions can help policymakers remember the past. The ultimate lesson of the League's experience, however, may be that institutions can be truly useful when they are encouraged to combine memory with a capacity to question reigning orthodoxies.

References

Adler, Emanuel, and Peter Haas, "Epistemic Communities, World Order, and the Creation of a Reflective Research Program," *International Organization*, 46 (No. 1, 1992), pp. 367–390.

Angell, Norman, *The Economic Functions of the League*, London, League of Nations Union, 1920.

Black, Stanley W., *A Levite among the Priests: Edward M. Bernstein and the Origins of the Bretton Woods System*, Boulder, Colo., Westview, 1991.

Brooks, Stephen, and Alain Gagnon, eds., *Social Scientists, Policy, and the State*, Westport, Conn., Praeger, 1990.

————, *The Political Influence of Ideas: Policy Communities and the Social Sciences*, Westport, Conn., Praeger, 1994.

Bryant, Ralph, "International Cooperation in the Making of National Macroeconomic Policies: Where Do We Stand?" in Peter B. Kenen, ed., *Understanding Interdependence: The Macroeconomics of the Open Economy*, Princeton, N.J., Princeton University Press, 1995, pp. 391–447.

————, *International Coordination of National Stabilization Policies*, Washington, D.C., Brookings Institution, 1996.

Clark, Ian D., "Should the IMF Become More Adaptive?" International Monetary Fund Working Paper 96/17, Washington, D.C., International Monetary Fund, February 1996.

Clarke, Stephen V.O., *Central Bank Cooperation, 1924–1931*, New York, Federal Reserve Bank of New York, 1967.

Cohen, Benjamin J., "The Triad and the Unholy Trinity: Lessons for the Pacific Region," in Richard Higgott, Richard Leaver, and John Ravenhill, eds., *Pacific Economic Relations in the 1990s*, London, Allen & Unwin, 1993.

Cooper, Richard N., Barry Eichengreen, C. Randall Henning, Gerald Holtham, and Robert Putnam, *Can Nations Agree? Issues in International Economic Cooperation*, Washington, D.C., Brookings Institution, 1989.

Cottrell, Philip, "Anglo-French Co-operation, 1850–1880," *Journal of European Economic History*, 3 (No. 1, 1974), pp. 54–86.

de Marchi, Neil, "League of Nations Economists and the Ideal of Peaceful Change in the Decade of the 'Thirties," in Craufurd D. Goodwin, ed., *Economics and National Security*, Durham, N.C., Duke University Press, 1991, pp. 143–178.

Dobson, Wendy, *Economic Policy Coordination: Requiem or Prologue?* Policy Analyses in International Economics No. 30, Washington, D.C., Institute for International Economics, 1991.

Dornbusch, Rudiger, *Post-Communist Monetary Problems: Lessons from the End of the Austro-Hungarian Empire*, San Francisco, Calif., ICS, 1994.

Dunham, Arthur, *The Anglo-French Treaty of 1860 and the Progress of the Industrial Revolution in France*, Ann Arbor, University of Michigan Press, 1930.

Eichengreen, Barry, *Elusive Stability: Essays in the History of International Finance, 1919–1939*, New York, Cambridge University Press, 1990.

———, *Golden Fetters: The Gold Standard and the Great Depression, 1919–1939*, New York, Oxford University Press, 1992.

———, *International Monetary Arrangements for the 21st Century*, Washington, D.C., Brookings Institution, 1995.

Eichengreen, Barry, and Peter Lindert, eds., *The International Debt Crisis in Historical Perspective*, Cambridge, Mass., MIT Press, 1989.

Eichengreen, Barry, and Jeffrey Sachs, "Exchange Rates and Economic Recovery in the 1930s," *Journal of Economic History*, 45 (December 1985), pp. 925–946.

Eichengreen, Barry, and Marc Uzan, "The 1933 World Economic Conference as an Instance of Failed International Collaboration," in Peter B. Evans, Harold K. Jacobson, Robert D. Putnam, eds., *Double-Edged Diplomacy: International Bargaining and Domestic Politics*, Berkeley, University of California Press, 1993, pp. 171–206.

Finnemore, Martha, "International Organizations as Teachers of Norms," *International Organization*, 47 (No. 4, 1993), pp. 565–598;

Frenkel, Jacob A., and Morris Goldstein, eds., *International Financial Policy: Essays in Honor of Jacques J. Polak*, Washington, D.C., International Monetary Fund, 1991.

Garber, Peter M., and Michael G. Spencer, *The Dissolution of the Austro-Hungarian Empire: Lessons for Currency Reform*, Essays in International Finance No. 191, Princeton, N.J., Princeton University, International Finance Section, February 1994.

Gold, Joseph, *Exchange Rates in International Law and Organization*, New York, American Bar Association, Section on International Law and Practice, 1988.

Goldstein, Judith, and Robert O. Keohane, eds., *Ideas and Foreign Policy: Beliefs, Institutions, and Political Change*, Ithaca, N.Y., Cornell University Press, 1993.

Granatstein, Jack Lawrence, "The Road to Bretton Woods: International Monetary Policy and the Public Servant," *Journal of Canadian Studies*, 16 (Fall-Winter 1981), pp. 174–187.

Guitián, Manuel, *Fund Conditionality*, Pamphlet Series No. 38, Washington, D.C., International Monetary Fund, 1981.

———, *Rules and Discretion in International Economic Policy*, Washington, D.C., International Monetary Fund, 1992a.

———, *The Unique Nature and the Responsibilities of the International Monetary Fund*, Pamphlet Series No. 46, Washington, D.C., International Monetary Fund, 1992b.

Haas, Ernst B., "Why Collaborate? Issue-Linkage and International Regimes," *World Politics*, 32 (April 1980) pp. 307–405.

———, *When Knowledge Is Power*, Berkeley, University of California Press, 1990.

Haberler, Gottfried von, *Prosperity and Depression*, 3rd ed., Geneva, League of Nations, 1941.

Hall, Peter A., ed., *The Political Power of Economic Ideas*, Princeton, N.J., Princeton University Press, 1989.

Helleiner, Eric, *States and the Reemergence of Global Finance*, Ithaca, N.Y., Cornell University Press, 1994.

Hill, Martin, *The Economic and Financial Organization of the League of Nations: A Survey of Twenty-Five Years' Experience*, Washington, D.C., Carnegie Endowment for International Peace, Division of International Law, Washington, 1945.

Huber, Ulrike, *Österreich und der Volkerbund in die 20er Jahren*, Ph.D. diss., University of Vienna, 1992.

Ikenberry, G. John, "A World Economy Restored: Expert Consensus and the Anglo-American Postwar Settlement," *International Organization*, 46 (No. 1, 1992), pp. 289–321.

———, "The Political Origins of Bretton Woods," in Michael Bordo and Barry Eichengreen, eds., *A Retrospective on the Bretton Woods System*, Chicago, University of Chicago Press, 1993, pp. 155–182

Ikenberry, G. John, and Charles A. Kupchan, "Socialization and Hegemonic Power," *International Organization*, 44 (No. 3, 1990), pp. 283–316.

International Financial Conference, "Report of the Conference, Brussels, September 24, 1920," League of Nations Archives, Economic and Financial Section, Box 503, Section 10a, Doc. 473, Geneva, United Nations Library, 1920.

Jacobsson, Erin E., *A Life for Sound Money*, Oxford, Clarendon, 1979.

Jacobsson, Per, *The Economic Consequences of the League*, London, Europa, 1927.

James, Harold, "The Historical Development of the Principle of Surveillance," *International Monetary Fund Staff Papers*, 42 (No. 4, 1995), pp. 762–791.

———, *International Monetary Cooperation Since Bretton Woods*, Washington, D.C., and New York, International Monetary Fund and Oxford University Press, 1996.

Kahler, Miles, *International Institutions and the Political Economy of Integration*, Washington, D.C., Brookings Institution, 1995.

Kapstein, Ethan, *Governing the Global Economy*, Cambridge, Mass., Harvard University Press, 1994.

Kenen, Peter, *The International Economy*, 3rd ed., Cambridge, Cambridge University Press, 1994.

———, ed., *Understanding Interdependence: The Macroeconomics of the Open Economy*, Princeton, N.J., Princeton University Press, 1995.

Keohane, Robert, *After Hegemony*, Princeton, N.J., Princeton University Press, 1984.

———, *International Institutions and State Power*, Boulder, Colo., Westview, 1989.

Keynes, John Maynard, "National Self-Sufficiency," *Yale Review*, 22 (No. 4, 1933), pp. 755–769.

———, *The General Theory of Employment, Interest, and Money*, London, Macmillan, 1936.

Kingdon, John W., *Agendas, Alternatives, and Public Policies*, Boston, Little, Brown, 1984.

Kunz, Diane, *The Battle for Britain's Gold Standard in 1931*, London, Croom Helm, 1987.

League of Nations, "Brussels Economic Conference, 1920: The Recommendations and Their Application: A Review After Two Years," League of Nations Archives, Economic and Financial Section, Doc. C.10.M.7.1923.II, Geneva, United Nations Library, 1922.

———, *Principles and Methods of Financial Reconstruction Work Undertaken under the Auspices of the League of Nations*, Geneva, League of Nations, 1930.

———, *Report of the Gold Delegation of the Financial Committee* (Archives Doc. II.A.12), Geneva, League of Nations, 1932.

———, Fiscal Committee, *Report to the Council on the Work of the Ninth Session of the Committee*, Geneva, League of Nations, June 12–21, 1939.

———, *Report of the Delegation on Economic Depressions, Part I: The Transition from War to Peace Economy*, Geneva, League of Nations, 1943.

———, *Report of the Delegation on Economic Depressions,. Part II: Economic Stability in the Post-War World: The Conditions of Prosperity After the Transition from War to Peace*, Geneva, League of Nations, 1945.

Loveday, Alexander, "The Economic and Financial Activities of the League," *International Affairs*, 17 (November, 1938), pp. 788–808.

McClure, Wallace, *World Prosperity As Sought through the Economic Work of the League of Nations*, New York, Macmillan, 1933.

Meyer, Richard Hemmig, *Bankers' Diplomacy: Monetary Stabilization in the Twenties*, New York, Columbia University Press, 1970.

Mills, J. Saxon, *The Genoa Conference*, London, Hutchison, 1922.

Monnet, Jean, *Memoirs*, London, Collins, 1978.

Murphy, Craig N., *International Organization and Industrial Change: Global Governance Since 1850*, New York, Oxford University Press, 1994.

Nixon, Frank, "Memorandum," League of Nations Archives, Economic and Financial Section, S.123, Doc. 16/2, Geneva, United Nations Library, August 1922.

Northedge, Frederick Samuel, *The League of Nations: Its Life and Times, 1920–1946*, New York, Holmes & Meier, 1986.

Norton, Joseph Jude, ed., "Section's Tribute to Sir Joseph Gold," *International Lawyer*, Special Issue, 23 (No. 4, 1989).

Nurkse, Ragnar, *International Currency Experience: Lessons of the Inter-War Period*, Geneva, League of Nations, 1944.

Odell, John S., "From London to Bretton Woods: Sources of Change in Bargaining Strategies and Outcomes," *Journal of Public Policy*, 8 (No. 3/4, 1988), pp. 287–315.

Oye, Kenneth, *Economic Discrimination and Political Exchange*, Princeton, N.J., Princeton University Press, 1992.

Pauly, Louis W., *Opening Financial Markets: Banking Politics on the Pacific Rim*, Ithaca, N.Y., Cornell University Press, 1988.

———, "The Political Foundations of Multilateral Economic Surveillance," *International Journal*, 47 (No. 2, 1992), pp. 293–327.

———, *Who Elected the Bankers? Surveillance and Control in the World Economy*, Ithaca, N.Y., Cornell University Press, forthcoming 1997.

Pauly, Louis W., and Janice Gross Stein, eds., *Choosing to Cooperate: How States Avoid Loss*, Baltimore, Md., Johns Hopkins University Press, 1993.

Plumptre, Arthur F.W., *Three Decades of Decision: Canada and the World Monetary System, 1944–75*, Toronto, McClelland and Stewart, 1977.

Polak, Jacques J., "The International Propagation of Business Cycles," *Review of Economic Studies*, 6 (February, 1939), pp. 79–99.

———, *The Changing Nature of IMF Conditionality*, Essays in International Finance, No. 184, Princeton, N.J., Princeton University, International Finance Section, 1991.

———, "The Internationalization of Economics: The Contribution of the International Monetary Fund," paper presented at Duke University, Durham, N.C., April 7–9, 1995a.

———, "Fifty Years of Exchange Rate Research and Policy at the International Monetary Fund," *International Monetary Fund Staff Papers*, 42 (No. 4, 1995b), pp. 734–761.

Ratcliffe, Barrie, "Napoleon III and the Anglo-French Commercial Treaty of 1860: A Reconsideration," *Journal of European Economic History*, 2 (No. 3, 1973), pp. 582–613.

Rogoff, Kenneth, "Can International Monetary Policy Cooperation Be Counterproductive?" *Journal of International Economics*, 18 (May, 1985), pp. 199–217.

Ruggie, John Gerard, "International Responses to Technology," *International Organization*, 29 (Summer 1975), pp. 557–584.

———, "International Regimes, Transactions, and Change: Embedded Liberalism in the Postwar Economic Order," *International Organization*, 36 (No. 2, 1982), pp. 379–415.

———, "Embedded Liberalism Revisited," in Emanuel Adler and Beverly Crawford, eds., *Progress in Postwar International Relations*, New York, Columbia University Press, 1991, pp. 201–234.

———, ed., *Multilateralism Matters*, New York, Columbia University Press, 1993.

———, "Trade, Protectionism and the Future of Welfare Capitalism," *Journal of International Affairs*, 48 (No. 2, 1994), pp. 1–13.

Salter, James Arthur, *Memoirs of a Public Servant*, London, Faber and Faber, 1961.

Santaella, Julio A., "Stabilization Programs and External Enforcement: Experience from the 1920s," *International Monetary Fund Staff Papers, 40 (No. 3, 1993), pp. 584–621.*

Schloss, Hans, *The Bank for International Settlements*, Amsterdam, North-Holland, 1958.

Schuker, Stephen A., *American "Reparations" to Germany 1919–33: Implications for the Third-World Debt Crisis*, Princeton Studies in International Finance No. 61, Princeton, N.J., Princeton University, International Finance Section, July 1988.

Scott, George, *The Rise and Fall of the League of Nations*, New York, Macmillan, 1973.

Simmons, Beth, "Why Innovate? Founding the Bank for International Settlements," *World Politics*, 45 (No. 3, 1993), pp. 361–405.

———, *Who Adjusts? Domestic Sources of Foreign Economic Policy During the Interwar Years*, Princeton, N.J., Princeton University Press, 1994.

Skidelsky, Robert, *John Maynard Keynes: The Economist As Savior, 1920–1937*, New York, Penguin, 1992.

Solomon, Robert, *Partners in Prosperity*, New York, Priority Press, 1991.

Strange, Susan, "IMF: Monetary Managers," in Robert Cox, Harold Jacobson et al., *The Anatomy of Influence*, New Haven, Yale University Press, 1973, pp. 263–297.

Temin, Peter, *Lessons from the Great Depression*, Cambridge, Mass., MIT Press, 1989.

Tinbergen, Jan, *Statistical Testing of Business Cycle Theories, Volume I: A Method and Its Application to Investment Activity*, Geneva, League of Nations, 1939a.

———, *Statistical Testing of Business Cycle Theories, Volume II: Business Cycles in the United States of America, 1919–1932*, Geneva, League of Nations, 1939b.

Toynbee, Arnold, *Survey of International Affairs, 1920–23*, Oxford, Oxford University Press, 1925.

Tyler, Royall, *The League of Nations Reconstruction Schemes in the Inter-War Period*, Geneva, League of Nations, 1945.

U.S. Department of State, *Foreign Relations of the United States*, Vol. 1, Washington, D.C., Government Printing Office, 1933.

Walters, Francis P., *A History of the League of Nations*, London, Oxford University Press, 1952.

Webb, Michael, *The Political Economy of Policy Coordination: International Adjustment Since 1945*, Ithaca, Cornell University Press, 1995.

Yee, Albert, "The Causal Effects of Ideas on Policies," *International Organization*, 50 (No. 1, 1996), pp. 69–108.

PUBLICATIONS OF THE
INTERNATIONAL FINANCE SECTION

Notice to Contributors

The International Finance Section publishes papers in four series: ESSAYS IN INTERNATIONAL FINANCE, PRINCETON STUDIES IN INTERNATIONAL FINANCE, and SPECIAL PAPERS IN INTERNATIONAL ECONOMICS contain new work not published elsewhere. REPRINTS IN INTERNATIONAL FINANCE reproduce journal articles previously published by Princeton faculty members associated with the Section. The Section welcomes the submission of manuscripts for publication under the following guidelines:

ESSAYS are meant to disseminate new views about international financial matters and should be accessible to well-informed nonspecialists as well as to professional economists. Technical terms, tables, and charts should be used sparingly; mathematics should be avoided.

STUDIES are devoted to new research on international finance, with preference given to empirical work. They should be comparable in originality and technical proficiency to papers published in leading economic journals. They should be of medium length, longer than a journal article but shorter than a book.

SPECIAL PAPERS are surveys of research on particular topics and should be suitable for use in undergraduate courses. They may be concerned with international trade as well as international finance. They should also be of medium length.

Manuscripts should be submitted in triplicate, typed single sided and double spaced throughout on 8½ by 11 white bond paper. Publication can be expedited if manuscripts are computer keyboarded in WordPerfect 5.1 or a compatible program. Additional instructions and a style guide are available from the Section.

How to Obtain Publications

The Section's publications are distributed free of charge to college, university, and public libraries and to nongovernmental, nonprofit research institutions. Eligible institutions may ask to be placed on the Section's permanent mailing list.

Individuals and institutions not qualifying for free distribution may receive all publications for the calendar year for a subscription fee of $40.00. Late subscribers will receive all back issues for the year during which they subscribe. Subscribers should notify the Section promptly of any change in address, giving the old address as well as the new.

Publications may be ordered individually, with payment made in advance. ESSAYS and REPRINTS cost $8.00 each; STUDIES and SPECIAL PAPERS cost $11.00. An additional $1.50 should be sent for postage and handling within the United States, Canada, and Mexico; $1.75 should be added for surface delivery outside the region.

All payments must be made in U.S. dollars. Subscription fees and charges for single issues will be waived for organizations and individuals in countries where foreign-exchange regulations prohibit dollar payments.

Please address all correspondence, submissions, and orders to:

International Finance Section
Department of Economics, Fisher Hall
Princeton University
Princeton, New Jersey 08544-1021

49

List of Recent Publications

A complete list of publications may be obtained from the International Finance Section.

ESSAYS IN INTERNATIONAL FINANCE

168. Paul Mosley, *Conditionality as Bargaining Process: Structural-Adjustment Lending, 1980-86.* (October 1987)
169. Paul A. Volcker, Ralph C. Bryant, Leonhard Gleske, Gottfried Haberler, Alexandre Lamfalussy, Shijuro Ogata, Jesús Silva-Herzog, Ross M. Starr, James Tobin, and Robert Triffin, *International Monetary Cooperation: Essays in Honor of Henry C. Wallich.* (December 1987)
170. Shafiqul Islam, *The Dollar and the Policy-Performance-Confidence Mix.* (July 1988)
171. James M. Boughton, *The Monetary Approach to Exchange Rates: What Now Remains?* (October 1988)
172. Jack M. Guttentag and Richard M. Herring, *Accounting for Losses On Sovereign Debt: Implications for New Lending.* (May 1989)
173. Benjamin J. Cohen, *Developing-Country Debt: A Middle Way.* (May 1989)
174. Jeffrey D. Sachs, *New Approaches to the Latin American Debt Crisis.* (July 1989)
175. C. David Finch, *The IMF: The Record and the Prospect.* (September 1989)
176. Graham Bird, *Loan-Loss Provisions and Third-World Debt.* (November 1989)
177. Ronald Findlay, *The "Triangular Trade" and the Atlantic Economy of the Eighteenth Century: A Simple General-Equilibrium Model.* (March 1990)
178. Alberto Giovannini, *The Transition to European Monetary Union.* (November 1990)
179. Michael L. Mussa, *Exchange Rates in Theory and in Reality.* (December 1990)
180. Warren L. Coats, Jr., Reinhard W. Furstenberg, and Peter Isard, *The SDR System and the Issue of Resource Transfers.* (December 1990)
181. George S. Tavlas, *On the International Use of Currencies: The Case of the Deutsche Mark.* (March 1991)
182. Tommaso Padoa-Schioppa, ed., with Michael Emerson, Kumiharu Shigehara, and Richard Portes, *Europe After 1992: Three Essays.* (May 1991)
183. Michael Bruno, *High Inflation and the Nominal Anchors of an Open Economy.* (June 1991)
184. Jacques J. Polak, *The Changing Nature of IMF Conditionality.* (September 1991)
185. Ethan B. Kapstein, *Supervising International Banks: Origins and Implications of the Basle Accord.* (December 1991)
186. Alessandro Giustiniani, Francesco Papadia, and Daniela Porciani, *Growth and Catch-Up in Central and Eastern Europe: Macroeconomic Effects on Western Countries.* (April 1992)
187. Michele Fratianni, Jürgen von Hagen, and Christopher Waller, *The Maastricht Way to EMU.* (June 1992)
188. Pierre-Richard Agénor, *Parallel Currency Markets in Developing Countries: Theory, Evidence, and Policy Implications.* (November 1992)
189. Beatriz Armendariz de Aghion and John Williamson, *The G-7's Joint-and-Several Blunder.* (April 1993)

190. Paul Krugman, *What Do We Need to Know About the International Monetary System?* (July 1993)

191. Peter M. Garber and Michael G. Spencer, *The Dissolution of the Austro-Hungarian Empire: Lessons for Currency Reform.* (February 1994)

192. Raymond F. Mikesell, *The Bretton Woods Debates: A Memoir.* (March 1994)

193. Graham Bird, *Economic Assistance to Low-Income Countries: Should the Link be Resurrected?* (July 1994)

194. Lorenzo Bini-Smaghi, Tommaso Padoa-Schioppa, and Francesco Papadia, *The Transition to EMU in the Maastricht Treaty.* (November 1994)

195. Ariel Buira, *Reflections on the International Monetary System.* (January 1995)

196. Shinji Takagi, *From Recipient to Donor: Japan's Official Aid Flows, 1945 to 1990 and Beyond.* (March 1995)

197. Patrick Conway, *Currency Proliferation: The Monetary Legacy of the Soviet Union.* (June 1995)

198. Barry Eichengreen, *A More Perfect Union? The Logic of Economic Integration.* (June 1996)

199. Peter B. Kenen, ed., with John Arrowsmith, Paul De Grauwe, Charles A. E. Goodhart, Daniel Gros, Luigi Spaventa, and Niels Thygesen, *Making EMU Happen—Problems and Proposals: A Symposium.* (August 1996)

200. Peter B. Kenen, ed., with Lawrence H. Summers, William R. Cline, Barry Eichengreen, Richard Portes, Arminio Fraga, and Morris Goldstein, *From Halifax to Lyons: What Has Been Done about Crisis Management?* (October 1996)

201. Louis W. Pauly, *The League of Nations and the Foreshadowing of the International Monetary Fund.* (December 1996)

PRINCETON STUDIES IN INTERNATIONAL FINANCE

59. Vincent P. Crawford, *International Lending, Long-Term Credit Relationships, and Dynamic Contract Theory.* (March 1987)

60. Thorvaldur Gylfason, *Credit Policy and Economic Activity in Developing Countries with IMF Stabilization Programs.* (August 1987)

61. Stephen A. Schuker, *American "Reparations" to Germany, 1919-33: Implications for the Third-World Debt Crisis.* (July 1988)

62. Steven B. Kamin, *Devaluation, External Balance, and Macroeconomic Performance: A Look at the Numbers.* (August 1988)

63. Jacob A. Frenkel and Assaf Razin, *Spending, Taxes, and Deficits: International-Intertemporal Approach.* (December 1988)

64. Jeffrey A. Frankel, *Obstacles to International Macroeconomic Policy Coordination.* (December 1988)

65. Peter Hooper and Catherine L. Mann, *The Emergence and Persistence of the U.S. External Imbalance, 1980-87.* (October 1989)

66. Helmut Reisen, *Public Debt, External Competitiveness, and Fiscal Discipline in Developing Countries.* (November 1989)

67. Victor Argy, Warwick McKibbin, and Eric Siegloff, *Exchange-Rate Regimes for a Small Economy in a Multi-Country World.* (December 1989)

68. Mark Gersovitz and Christina H. Paxson, *The Economies of Africa and the Prices of Their Exports*. (October 1990)
69. Felipe Larraín and Andrés Velasco, *Can Swaps Solve the Debt Crisis? Lessons from the Chilean Experience*. (November 1990)
70. Kaushik Basu, *The International Debt Problem, Credit Rationing and Loan Pushing: Theory and Experience*. (October 1991)
71. Daniel Gros and Alfred Steinherr, *Economic Reform in the Soviet Union: Pas de Deux between Disintegration and Macroeconomic Destabilization*. (November 1991)
72. George M. von Furstenberg and Joseph P. Daniels, *Economic Summit Declarations, 1975-1989: Examining the Written Record of International Cooperation*. (February 1992)
73. Ishac Diwan and Dani Rodrik, *External Debt, Adjustment, and Burden Sharing: A Unified Framework*. (November 1992)
74. Barry Eichengreen, *Should the Maastricht Treaty Be Saved?* (December 1992)
75. Adam Klug, *The German Buybacks, 1932-1939: A Cure for Overhang?* (November 1993)
76. Tamim Bayoumi and Barry Eichengreen, *One Money or Many? Analyzing the Prospects for Monetary Unification in Various Parts of the World*. (September 1994)
77. Edward E. Leamer, *The Heckscher-Ohlin Model in Theory and Practice*. (February 1995)
78. Thorvaldur Gylfason, *The Macroeconomics of European Agriculture*. (May 1995)
79. Angus S. Deaton and Ronald I. Miller, *International Commodity Prices, Macroeconomic Performance, and Politics in Sub-Saharan Africa*. (December 1995)
80. Chander Kant, *Foreign Direct Investment and Capital Flight*. (April 1996)
81. Gian Maria Milesi-Ferretti and Assaf Razin, *Current-Account Sustainability*. (October 1996)

SPECIAL PAPERS IN INTERNATIONAL ECONOMICS

16. Elhanan Helpman, *Monopolistic Competition in Trade Theory*. (June 1990)
17. Richard Pomfret, *International Trade Policy with Imperfect Competition*. (August 1992)
18. Hali J. Edison, *The Effectiveness of Central-Bank Intervention: A Survey of the Literature After 1982*. (July 1993)
19. Sylvester W.C. Eijffinger and Jakob De Haan, *The Political Economy of Central-Bank Independence*. (May 1996)

REPRINTS IN INTERNATIONAL FINANCE

28. Peter B. Kenen, *Ways to Reform Exchange-Rate Arrangements*; reprinted from *Bretton Woods: Looking to the Future*, 1994. (November 1994)
29. Peter B. Kenen, *Sorting Out Some EMU Issues*; reprinted from Jean Monnet Chair Paper 38, Robert Schuman Centre, European University Institute, 1996. (December 1996)